LLOYD LOOM

The Lloyd Loom
'Around this famous loom which revolutionized the weaving industry
is built the interesting story of Lloyd Loom Products'
(Lloyd's 1920s Catalogue)

LLOYD LOOM
woven fibre furniture

Lee J. Curtis

PUBLISHED BY
SALAMANDER BOOKS LIMITED
LONDON

Dedicated to Victor and Violet

Endpapers: Lloyd Loom armchairs furnishing the observation lounge of the airship R100, c.1929. *Hulton Deutsch collection.*

Page i: 'Happy baby in a Lloyd', c.1928.
Page iii: 1920s artwork for Lusty's Lloyd Loom catalogue cover.

A SALAMANDER BOOK

Published by Salamander Books Ltd
8 Blenheim Court, Brewery Road
London N7 9NT
United Kingdom

© Salamander Books Ltd 1991

This (revised) edition
© Salamander Books Ltd 1997, 2000

A member of the Chrysalis Group plc

ISBN 0 86101 940 7

All correspondence concerning the content of this volume should be addressed to Salamander Books Ltd.

CREDITS
Editor: Richard Collins
Designer: Lee J. Curtis
Art editor: Mark Holt
Typesetter: Ian Palmer
Photographers: Peter Wood (UK, location and studio), Val Ide (USA, location)
Colour reproduction: P & W Graphics, Singapore
Printed and bound in Spain

AUTHOR'S NOTE
In the six years since this book was first published, pre-war Lloyd Loom furniture has continued to boom in popularity and, consequently, it has become much more difficult to find. I would have expected, for example, to discover several of Lusty's Delux model chairs during a weekend tour of London's antique shops and market places back in 1991 (page 151). I would be lucky to find one exceptional piece now in a month of touring. Dealers that previously stocked a selection of Lloyd Loom furniture now report that demand has outstripped supply and are exasperated by customers often reluctant to pay the premium prices that the better pieces now command. This should not, however, discourage anyone wishing to purchase a really fine old piece of Lloyd Loom. The hunt may take longer but it will be all the more rewarding for this. Prices may now appear high to dealers and collectors that were purchasing vintage Lloyd Loom in the 1980s but this is because the furniture was grossly undervalued at that time and not because it is expensive now. For its uniqueness, versatility and historical interest, Lloyd Loom still represents excellent value for money. Real bargains, rare and exceptional pieces, can still be found and will continue to emerge for many years to come. Fine old Lloyd Loom may no longer be priced just as second-hand furniture, but the subject as a serious field of collecting for investment, as well as pleasure, has perhaps only just begun.

Lee J. Curtis
Munich, January 1997

AUTHOR'S ACKNOWLEDGMENTS
Special thanks to Don and Dudley Flanders, Gene Davenport, David Lemerond, and all at Lloyd/Flanders, the people of Menominee and Marinette, Bob and Dinah Meissner, Betty Furlong, Don Larsen, Geoffrey Lusty, Will Lusty, Sarah Lusty, Harriet Wiseman, George Barber, George Gray, David and Kim Breese, Peter Unützer, Stephanie Seidl, and the many antiques dealers and friends who helped make this book a pleasure to research.

The author will be grateful to receive comments from collectors that may improve further editions of this book.

CONTENTS

Page 7
NEITHER CANE NOR WICKER?

Page 13
1 MARSHALL BURNS LLOYD

Page 23
2 THE MAKERS OF VINTAGE LLOYD LOOM

Page 45
3 MAKING LLOYD LOOM

Page 67
4 VINTAGE PRODUCTS, 1920–1940

Page 123
5 DATING LLOYD LOOM

Page 143
6 CARE, REPAIR AND ASSESSING VALUE

Page 158
INDEX

Page 160
APPENDIX

NEITHER CANE NOR WICKER?

In 1922 a new type of furniture appeared in Britain with the legend 'NEITHER CANE NOR WICKER – SUPERIOR TO EITHER'! It bore a trade mark, already famous in America, which was about to become a household name in Great Britain. The furniture appeared to be similar to fine, traditional hand-crafted wicker but was woven with a wonderful new fibre 'impervious', it claimed, 'to damp and dirt'. It was 'hygienic' and it did not 'warp'; it was 'unaffected by heat'. The trade mark was 'Lloyd Loom' and the new wonder fibre was, quite simply, paper.

Lloyd Loom was to become one of the most successful products of the twentieth century. It created a new consumer radical, pioneered modern factory production techniques and left a legacy of over 1000 individual furniture designs. Over 10 million pieces of Lloyd Loom would be made in America and Britain before 1940. It furnished great mansions and modest homes, hotels, restaurants, tea rooms, luxurious ocean liners and even airships.

What made this furniture so special that it merited such success? The answer to this lies only partly in the fact that Lloyd Loom appears similar to the very finest hand-crafted wicker; it has all the advantages of traditional wicker but none of the disadvantages. Lloyd Loom is, strictly speaking, a wicker product but it was sufficiently different to create a new market. It was more than improved wicker; it was a new type of furniture and although it captured a massive share of the market for traditional wicker it also sold to a market which would not have purchased wicker had Lloyd Loom not existed.

Lloyd Loom furniture is smooth to the touch, with no sharp joints in the weave which can snag clothing. It does not bend, distort or creak when used. It is remarkably strong and durable and, if cared for, will show few signs of wear even after decades of constant use. Pieces of Lloyd Loom furniture, in daily use since 1922, are now still as good as new.

'Lloyd Loom' derives from the surname of its American inventor, Marshall Burns Lloyd, who, in 1917, patented a new system for the manufacture of wicker products. Lloyd did not invent a 'loom' in 1917 and neither did he initiate the use of paper in manufacturing furniture. Twisted kraft paper, or 'art fibre', had been developed in the early 1900s as a cheaper and more readily available material for wicker production, and was extensively used during the First World War when the shipping of other traditional materials such as rattan and cane was disrupted.

Because the furniture buying public would not have recognised paper as a durable material, the term 'woven fibre' was employed to explain the product. And the paper, tightly twisted into a twine, was partly reinforced with strands of steel wire.

Left: A very rare Lusty's Lloyd Loom armchair with double-sided arms and a separated skirt, c.1922. *Collection of the Anacara Company, Stamford, CT, USA.*

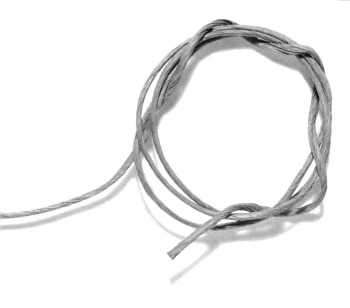

Above: 'The total weight of the four men standing on the piece of Lloyd fibre fabric pictured above is 577 pounds. Hundreds of pounds more could easily be held up by this fabric because of its steel centre reinforcement.' *Lloyd's Catalogue, 1938.*

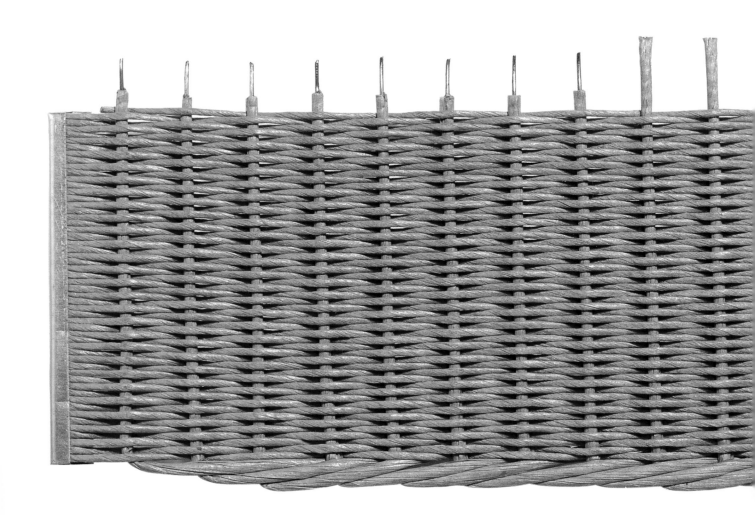

Above: Illustration used as a logo for Art Fibre products made for the homecraft market by Grand Rapids Fibre Co., Grand Rapids, Mich., USA. This company sold a wide range of pre-war weaving aids and self-construction kits that used Art Fibre – 'a paper cord of unusual strength, similar in appearance to traditional reed, but far more flexible and easier to handle'.

Left: A section of Lloyd Loom woven fibre material (without paint finish) that shows how the fabric is constructed.
The vertical strands are known as 'stakes' and contain wire – visible at the top of the section – where the paper that covers them has been peeled back.
The horizontal strands are known as 'filler strands' and are made of twisted paper (art fibre) without wire.
Stake ends at the lower edge of the section are plaited back to contain the filler strands and facilitate nailing or stapling of the edge to a frame. The metal strip (left edge) clamps the ends of the filler strands to prevent fraying. This is nailed to the frame but usually hidden or covered by decorative braid.

Right: A typical decorative 'figure of eight' braid, woven out of fibre strands and used to cover the edge of the Lloyd Loom material where it is nailed to the framework.

RECOGNISING LLOYD LOOM

All Lloyd Loom furniture is constructed from this twisted paper and wire material which is nailed onto, not woven around, the framework. Other types of fibre furniture were made, both traditionally hand-woven or, as in the case of Lloyd Loom, mechanically produced, but only Lloyd Loom included wire in its fine, tightly woven products. This is significant because, where Lloyd Loom has survived the passing of time and the rigours of daily use, the majority of its unwired competitors have fallen apart and disappeared.

There is a very simple way to distinguish Lloyd Loom from lookalike fibre copies. A strong magnet does the job in seconds: it will only stick to Lloyd Loom weave because of the steel wire in the stakes. Alternatively, you can look for the wire in the stake ends which are usually plaited down on the underside of larger items such as chairs. These will be pin sharp, so beware if you poke them with your fingers; they are normally well hidden or covered with a woven braid.

You can recognise Lloyd Loom, too, by the general resilience of the material which will be firm to the touch yet with a slight springiness. And, unless the item has been heavily painted, it is usually possible to discern the paper material by its tightly twisted pattern. If you tore a strip of paper and hand twisted it into a string it would look similar.

Cane, rattan and other traditional wicker materials are naturally limited in length and joins may be apparent in the weave. Fibre strands were produced in endless coils so that joins are very rare. Lloyd Loom woven fibre is always nailed onto a separately produced frame. Traditional hand-crafted wicker is woven around the frame and cannot be separated from the frame construction. Other makes of furniture were produced in America using wired fibre but these generally used a much heavier gauge material which was woven around the frame and not produced on a loom.

The simplest way to recognise genuine Lloyd Loom is to look for the original 'Lloyd Loom' trade mark. The majority of items produced were labelled and these labels can often be found intact on the underside of an item. An explanation and catalogue of labels appear in the chapter on dating.

The Lloyd Loom material and construction technique created a distinct style which is clearly illustrated in this book; although other lookalike (unwired) copies exist, it is by far the most popular of all pre-war 'woven fibre' furniture. I have attempted here to explain what Lloyd Loom is by illustrating how the material differs from other products, but such an explanation does not adequately define 'Lloyd Loom'. How it was invented, who made it and how it was manufactured is explained in the following chapters. There are many reasons why this furniture became successful, some of which have little to do with the method by which it was constructed. These will become apparent as you read and, I hope, enjoy the book.

Lloyd Loom furniture was established before the Wall Street crash of 1929 but it thrived during the years of the Great Depression that followed. It had a certain quality which endeared it to people even during those difficult times; that quality is now being recognised and rediscovered by a different generation. Although Lloyd Loom is not made of cane it is wicker. But, then again, it was a new type of wicker, and as such deserved a new name.

Left: A 1930s Lusty's newspaper advertisement. Their Lloyd Loom products became massively popular in the 1930s and were sold in over 8000 retail outlets throughout Great Britain.

Right: 'In how few gardens can one sit in real comfort? Yet when the weather is hot and the view shimmers in the heat, sink into a Lloyd Loom chair and you'll find restfulness in its deep comfort. Its gay colourings, too, are in keeping with a warm summer afternoon . . .' Opening text to accompany this illustration, one of the earliest British Lloyd Loom full page colour advertisements, which appeared in the *Ideal Home* magazine, August 1930.

INTO THE WICKER MARKET

The mechanisation of Lloyd's process soon made his company the largest recognised producer of baby carriages and prams in the world. His products were shipped to every corner of the United States and the spread of his Lloyd Loom products set off alarm bells in the wicker industry. It was clear that once the system was set up to produce furniture the long established traditional wicker makers would be in for a hard time. This was compounded by the fact that Lloyd's products closely resembled the very finest and most costly hand-woven wicker items yet had none of the problems inherent in the use of traditional materials. The Washburn & Heywood Chair Company, a massive, highly respectable and long established manufacturer of hand-crafted wicker, saw the writing on the wall and in 1921 consolidated into a new company and made Lloyd an offer he could not refuse. Lloyd Manufacturing became part of the newly incorporated Heywood-Wakefield Company, leaving Lloyd largely independent within his company but with increased capital and a valuable entrée into the furniture business.

Lloyd explained why he was initially detained from making furniture in an article published by the *Lloyd Shop News*, a newspaper printed monthly by and for his employees: 'I saw the possibilities of that [furniture] industry early in the game but it took time to develop. We were crowded for space because of the carriage demand. We did some building, but even then we needed that room so that we could make more carriages. Finally we did make some furniture. It was an experiment but we felt pretty certain it was going across as well as the carriages. Our salesmen put the furniture on the market. Naturally there was some criticism. Some of the pieces were a little too crude, so we improved them and last year [1922] we came forth with our complete line of perfected furniture'.

AFTER THE LOOM

By 1923, the year in which he announced a massive building programme to improve production of his successful furniture products, Lloyd was sixty-five years old. He had divorced a second time and re-married at the age of sixty and was, as always, constantly working on new ideas. In 1924 he retired from managing the Menominee factory but remained a director of Heywood-Wakefield with the additional, rather grand title 'Advisory Engineer to the Corporation'. Increasingly plagued by ill-health, Lloyd nevertheless maintained his own independent experimental workshop close to his Menominee home which employed a dozen men.

He had a vision of a new town with homes affordable to the factory workers – pre-fabricated houses built with the new insulation techniques he was developing. He interrupted this project, shortly before his death, to involve himself in other community building projects which were deemed more urgent.

Lloyd had always been actively committed to local politics and community projects. He had served twice as Mayor of Menominee in 1913 and 1917, and, carrying his creative talent into local politics, had become known as 'Efficiency Lloyd'. He was responsible for a wide range of social projects, some of which he personally funded – such as the securing of a clean public water supply, the building of a local theatre, a department store and later, through a bequest, a hospital.

Marshall Burns Lloyd, credited with over 200 inventions, died on 10 August 1927. He left an estate worth more than two million dollars which, but for his personal eccentricity and generosity, would no doubt have been a much larger fortune. It would be wrong to assume that Lloyd's wicker production invention – the separation of the construction of the frame and the weave – could just as easily have been devised by someone else. An entire industry had taken thousands of years to find such a 'simple' solution; but for Lloyd, it might not have been realised even to this day.

Above: Lloyd's mausoleum in Menominee which reflected his importance to the local community. It was planned and built for him by his friends who reported to a local newspaper the day after his death was announced, 'It will be a stately sepulchral monument on a hill overlooking the entrance to Riverside [cemetery]. It is a beautiful spot'.

TWO

THE MAKERS
OF VINTAGE LLOYD LOOM

Lloyd Loom furniture was produced largely at the Menominee factory, but it was also manufactured elsewhere in the United States as well as in other countries, under licence from Lloyd. The majority of other such outlets are insignificant, with the exception of one: W. Lusty & Sons, of London. The English company, owned and run by the Lusty family, produced a considerable range of Lloyd Loom furniture between the wars and firmly established its name in Europe.

In 1921, Lloyd had sold his manufacturing works to Heywood-Wakefield and with it the rights to produce Lloyd Loom in the United States. Although the furniture would be developed and made at Menominee, still under Lloyd's guidance, Heywood-Wakefield would play a significant part in putting the product on to the market and establishing its place there. One of America's oldest and most respected furniture manufacturers, Heywood-Wakefield owned several factories, warehouses and showrooms throughout the United States and employed nearly 5000 staff. One of the company's first acts, on buying out Lloyd in 1921, was to take on production of his highly successful baby-carriage line, something with which it had been struggling to compete (with traditional hand-made wicker) since 1918. Furniture products, fully launched in 1922, also fell into line and were manufactured at factories in Chicago,

Left: A rare Lloyd Loom armchair, Lusty's Delux model No. 65 (c.1928–41) with rounded front skirt and ball leg detail. The example shown, from about 1928, is in its original colour with diamond weave pattern. *Private collection.*

at Gardner and Wakefield in Massachusetts, and in Canada, at Orillia, Ontario, to the east of Georgian Bay and Meaford where Lloyd grew up. The Canadian factory, coincidentally, was managed by Alfred Lloyd, a former employee at the Menominee plant and Marshall B. Lloyd's nephew.

SELLING LLOYD LOOM ABROAD

Although Lloyd had sold manufacturing rights in the United States to Heywood-Wakefield in 1921, he held foreign rights to his invention, and had already been looking abroad for buyers. His Lloyd Loom system had received wide coverage in the foreign press, through trade magazines and scientific journals, and after an article appeared in *La Nature* in 1920, French rights were sold to René Duval and Pierre Mouronval, both of whom were in the wicker business. Duval visited the Menominee factory and shipped machinery back to his factory in France in 1921 to make baby carriages, furniture and baskets for the French market. Rights, and machinery, were also sold to H.C. Tucker in 1920 for the markets in Australia and New Zealand, for furniture to be produced in Melbourne and Auckland respectively. History does not relate what happened to either enterprise and I have yet to discover any products which originate from these sources. Two 1930s photographs which appear in *The Fabulous Interiors of the Great Ocean Liners* by William H. Miller, Jr (Dover, 1985) illustrate the French Liners *Ile de France* and *Champlaine* with interiors furnished with 'considerable use of rattan and wood'. The furniture illustrated is, in my opinion, Lloyd Loom rather than rattan and I believe this to be connected to Messieurs Duval and Mouronval.

A factory was also established in Germany in about 1922, an enterprise organised by Lloyd with the aid of workers of German origin at the Menominee factory. The Lloyd-Sello Fibre Company at Fulda, near Frankfurt, was set up by Elof Klar, who had trained staff to operate machinery in Menominee. No doubt the factory was founded on a springboard of optimism following the First World War, but conditions then were still desperately hard in Germany. And yet, despite the economic situation, by 1923 the factory was producing furniture. A photograph of the factory's machine room, which appeared in the *Lloyd Shop News*, shows finished items in a loading bay which look identical to the furniture produced by Lloyd. George Fussner, another former Menominee employee, was left in charge of the factory and remained optimistic that the plant would be successful 'after conditions . . . returned to normal'. Apparently they did not return to the right sort of normality, for there is no mention of the German factory after November 1923.

There is a postscript to this. In 1988, a German collector of Lloyd Loom showed me some pieces he had purchased in Munich. At that time, I did not know about the Fulda plant, and felt that he was fortunate to have found such American-made Lloyd Loom in Europe, where it is something of a rarity. Perhaps the furniture had been shipped to Europe by an American family moving house or, and I now believe this to be more likely, it originated from the Lloyd-Sello plant at Fulda.

Although Lloyd Loom furniture was produced in other countries, it is certain that the output was small, minimal in comparison to Lusty's output. Lusty's dominated the British market; they produced millions of pieces from over 400 designs and shipped furniture all over the world to the then numerous British colonies. They were as prolific in Europe as Lloyd's were in America: together, both companies were responsible for the vast majority of Lloyd Loom furniture produced before 1940 which is now regarded as vintage Lloyd Loom. Both the American and British manufacturers are equally as important to the history of Lloyd Loom; each played a significant role in its design and marketing. Although similar, the character of the furniture reflects the different circumstances that existed on either side of the Atlantic.

Left: The machine room, Lloyd-Sello Fibre Company, Fulda, Germany, c.1923. Furniture similar to that produced in Menominee can be seen stacked by the doors leading to a loading bay.

Right: A Lloyd's rocking armchair, model No. 07, c.1928. *Private collection.*

Left: A collection of Lusty's Lloyd Loom photographed to illustrate a magazine article entitled 'The Lloyd Loom Revival', one of many pieces to have appeared in the press prompted by the return to popularity and escalation in price of old pieces of Lloyd Loom furniture. (Left to right) A model No. 7351 armchair, 1935–40; a child's rocking chair based on a 30s design but made in the 1950s; Model No. 162X, linen basket, 1933–40; model No. 158, (shoe) cupboard, 1930–40; model No. 27, armchair, 1927–40; model No. 137, occasional table, 1932–40; 1950s plant stand; model No. 85, armchair, 1922–40; and model No. 7074, pattern weave chair, 1935–40. *Good Housekeeping. Photograph: Huntley Hedworth.*

W. LUSTY & SONS

William Lusty started his business in 1872 from a small hardware shop in London's East End. A jack-of-all trades, he also developed a timber business by salvaging driftwood, fallen from barges, out of the local canal; by the turn of the century, this had become an important local, family industry which specialised in the manufacture and supply of wooden packing cases and beer crates. During the First World War, the company expanded its business by adapting to make munitions cases. By 1918 the business had vastly increased its manufacturing capacity and, with capital to invest, required a new product line.

The diversification into furniture production was typical of Lusty's canny opportunism. When a New York agent for their packing case business read about the Lloyd invention in the American trade journal *Packages,* and passed the information on to Lusty's, they were quick to show interest and act. They swiftly signed up the British rights and Frank Lusty arrived in America in May 1920 to acquaint himself with Lloyd's system. He stayed at Menominee for four months, during which time he worked on the factory floor, in each section of the plant, in order to obtain a thorough knowledge of the system. Full patent rights and the basic machinery were purchased in 1921 and Lusty's were in production by the following year. Lusty's and Lloyd's would never be in direct competition with each other; instead, they nurtured a friendly and mutually productive association in which development of ideas and designs for their furniture would be shared.

Above: Lusty's factory complex at Bromley-by-Bow, in the East End of London adjacent to docklands, a position that would become perilous in 1940 and catastrophic to the Lusty family. The canal was used to deliver extensive stocks of hardwood required for furniture and packing case production but the site was too congested to store finished furniture. The site, which nowadays houses several new industries, can still be identified although the railway sidings (top left) have disappeared and few of Lusty's buildings remain.

Left: William Lusty seated (far left) with his family on the occasion of his son William's wedding in 1915. Frank Lusty, who was to travel to Menominee to study Lloyd's manufacturing process, is pictured behind William, Jr., and between two of his other brothers, J.F. and Arch Lusty; all of them would be involved in the manufacture of British Lloyd Loom under licence from Lloyd's.

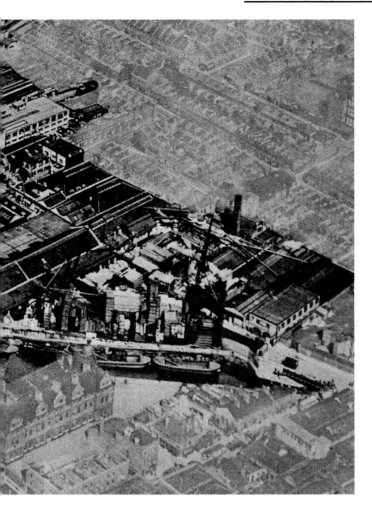

complimentary booklet, 'My trip thru the Lloyd plant', a touch that was as innovative and inventive in the early 1930s as the furniture it was endorsing. It is hard to imagine visitors to Lusty's completing a successful tour of their London factory. Nonetheless, despite the apparently chaotic layout, there was no disputing that this was as well equipped and as productive as Menominee.

LAUNCHING THE FURNITURE IN THE USA

The American market differed substantially from the British. Thanks to the overwhelming success of his baby carriages, Lloyd's market was ready made and established, his workforce well acquainted with the material and construction technique for making furniture. Lusty's had no such familiarity: they were starting from scratch with no previous experience in wicker production, no connection in the furniture retail trade and an unknown product.

Based as Lloyd's optimism was on solid manufacturing experience and knowledge of his market, he also did his sums. The possibilities of furniture production were discussed in a lengthy article in the October 1920 issue of the *Lloyd Shop News*. The article analysed the reasons for the success of the baby carriages and came up with the information that every one person in ninety-six in America was interested in baby carriages. If most families bought only

LUSTY'S LONDON FACTORY

The Lusty Lloyd Loom factory complex covered an area of about 17 acres at Bromley-by-Bow in the East End of London. Situated in a typically urban industrial environment it formed a triangular plot, bordered on one side by the Limehouse Cut, a tributary of the Grand Union Canal, with Empson Street and extensive railway sidings forming its other boundaries. The immediate area was a sprawl of densely packed rows of Victorian houses, where most of Lusty's employees lived, mixed with other local industry.

The contrast, therefore, between the American and British factories could not have been greater. The Menominee plant, purpose-built on a green site with plenty of room for expansion; Lusty's, by contrast, hemmed in, their works largely a confused mass of converted and poorly ordered buildings, without the scope for or possibility of any sort of expansion.

In America, the Menominee plant was a source of local pride. It was a local landmark and actually became a tourist attraction. Visitors were taken on guided tours and given a

Below and over: A Lloyd's pram parade, c.1922. IND, USA.

one carriage for an entire growing family – assuming that carriages were passed down the line – what then of the potential for selling furniture? It reasoned, not unnaturally, that demand for furniture was quite different and stated some quite remarkable statistical 'facts' with regard to this – 'One person in twenty four is a furniture buyer', and required to 'continually replace worn-out furniture . . . Every person wanting furniture needs from thirty to seventy-five pieces of which from six to twenty are made of wicker'! (One wonders how these figures were arrived at.) 'It must then follow,' it continued, 'that demand for wicker furniture is forty times greater than the demand for baby carriages' and that 'the demand for wicker is constantly increasing'. And in conclusion 'Hence, since the Lloyd company has been able to make such tremendous strides by the production of baby carriages alone, what will it do when it also pushes wicker furniture?'

One may perhaps assume that the analysis was somewhat exaggerated. It is now generally accepted that, far from 'constantly increasing', the popularity of wicker furniture (about 1920) was beginning to wane in America. Fancy and ornate wicker, so popular in the nineteenth century, had gone out of vogue. The industry was in the doldrums through failing to provide new styles. Lloyd Loom could provide the fine weave look which was associated with the highest quality wicker but, more important than this, it would mass produce new, simple but stylish forms. The 'Lloyd Loom' trademark was a powerful tool; it alone suggested something new, the word 'loom' being associated with the industrial age. 'Lloyd's New Wicker' might not have had the same impact.

Lloyd's figures should be taken with a pinch of salt. Although the furniture line was extremely successful and caused the Menominee factory to double its turnover, it would not have been possible for the company to have outstripped its baby-carriage production with furniture by anything like the 'forty times' potential that had been suggested. Quite simply, it could not have handled such an enormous rate of expansion, hence Lloyd's decision to join Heywood-Wakefield and to licence abroad. Lloyd Loom furniture was launched practically simultaneously in Britain and America in 1922. It was immediately successful in America but met with almost complete indifference in Britain.

Right: A page from Lauerman Brothers Co., Marinette, WI, store catalogue for 1926 (with 1926 prices). The catalogue illustrated three full pages of Lloyd Loom products, this one depicting the less expensive models. The page was captioned 'Furnish that library, living room or sun parlor with this beautiful low-priced Lloyd fibre suite . . . it gives you beauty at low cost and will make your home your greatest pride.' The items depicted represent some of the most popular designs produced in the 1920s by Lloyd's but are now quite difficult to find, especially in original colour.

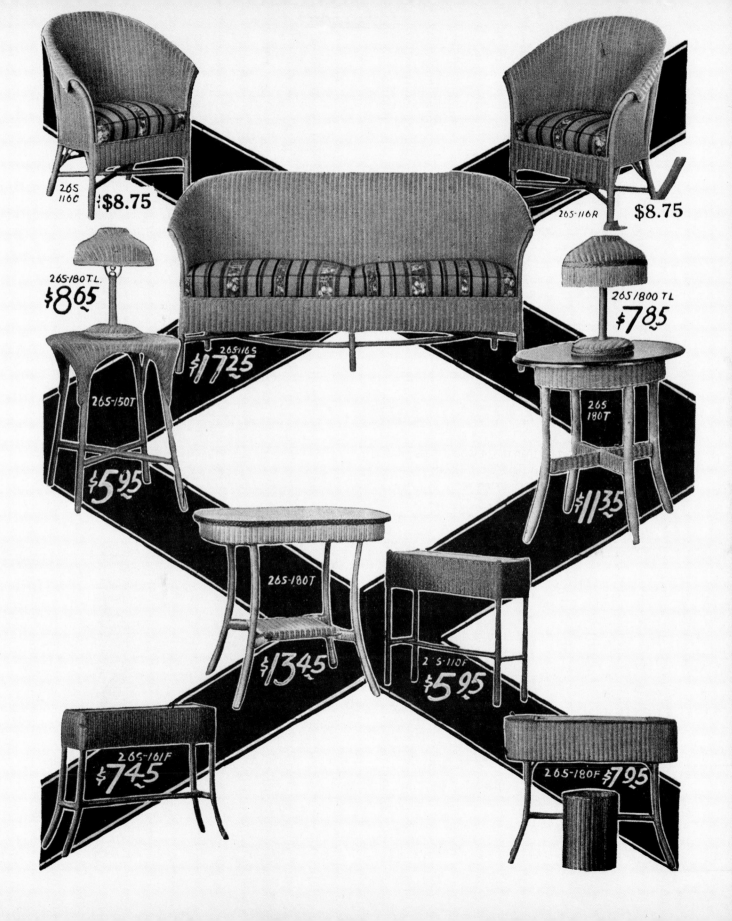

265
116C $8.75

265-116R $8.75

265-180 T.L.
$865

265-116 S
$1725

265-150T
$595

265/800 TL
$785

265
180T
$1135

265-180T
$1345

265-110F
$595

265-161F
$745

265-180F $795

LUSTY'S: SUCCESS AND NEAR FAILURE

Compared with the American product, the earliest British-made Lloyd Loom was less refined and somewhat rustic. Designs were based on a very simple construction technique made necessary by the presence of a relatively unskilled workforce. Because Lusty's had to establish product lines, maintain turnover *and* train their staff during the first two years, most of their furniture was based on square sections which did not require any complex shaping. (An example of Lusty's design and manufacturing technique during these early days is shown on page 138.) It illustrates that the simple elegance for which Lloyd Loom is now famous was not achieved overnight.

But Lusty's had problems far more serious than that of their manufacturing technique to contend with. By 1924, American sales exceeded three and a half million dollars; British sales were pitiful and Lusty's were on the verge of collapse. Despite refining their production techniques to produce furniture up to the standard of their American counterparts, the market was not responding. Britain did not have a great traditional wicker industry and wicker furniture had not naturally progressed into the home as it had in America. It was purchased only by the minority, invariably those wealthy enough to own conservatories, summer houses or large gardens. It was not regarded as suitable everyday living room furniture and its market, even as garden furniture, was confounded by the vagaries of the British climate.

Lusty's made great claims as to the excellence of their product and its superiority over traditional wicker, and their early advertisements tried to promote it as furniture 'which will harmonise perfectly with any scheme of interior decoration'. Reviews were good but only seemed to appear alongside those of bona fide garden furniture.

The development of the Lusty's factory for Lloyd Loom had required enormous financial investment. The loom process was an inexpensive one but only if used for mass-market production, which Lusty's still struggled to achieve. Accepting that they did not after all have a ready-made market, they concentrated on improving their product range, and issued a free booklet 'containing photographs of 30 useful designs'. *Ideal Home* magazine was the main outlet for their promotional campaign but in the main their advertisements were dull and uninspiring. Sales crawled up but still remained depressingly well below expectations. Lusty's fortunes began to change dramatically in 1929.

ROYDS' ADVERTISING CAMPAIGN

What changed them was, at last, a brilliantly conceived advertising campaign which would ultimately establish the product as a famous brand name and alter the British public's perception of wicker as nothing more than garden furniture. The Lustys were never masters of the art of advertising: the excellent campaign was the work of a professional agency, Royds, headed by George Royds. His brief was short: 'Bring our furniture into the home.'

Royds knew that a subtle approach to the Lusty campaign was essential. Sales could not be achieved simply by putting the furniture into a standard interior setting and

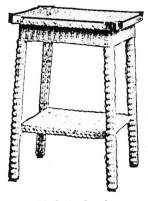

Ideal Furnishing on Dainty Lines.
LLOYD *LOOM* FURNITURE
Neither Cane nor Wicker—Superior to Either.

PERFECT IN FINISH AND EQUALLY SUITABLE FOR HOME OR GARDEN.

RELIABILITY of construction, unequalled durability and beauty of design, make Lloyd Loom Woven Furniture Absolutely the Best Value obtainable. Supplied in any colour desired.

HEAT, SUNSHINE & WEATHER PROOF.

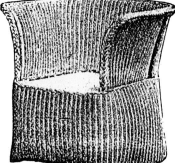

Made in London.

LLOYD LOOM FURNITURE *can be seen at most good class stores. Write to-day for illustrated leaflet and name of nearest agent to*

W. LUSTY & SONS (Dept. I), Bromley-by-Bow, E.3

Above: An early Lusty's magazine advertisement shown in *Ideal Home*, July 1923. It depicts an extremely rare version of their model No. 28 type armchair and an early table with woven fibre covered legs.

Right: Lusty's more complex model No. 5294 armchair with indented serpentine front skirt. This early model (c.1929) with diamond weave pattern is from the 'Delux' range produced between 1928 and 1940. It is now rare. *Collection of the Anacara Company, Stamford, CT, USA.*

trying to persuade people as to its rightful place there. The illustrated campaign would have to be cleverly angled in order to win public acceptance. Royds began by associating the furniture in people's minds with summer rather than the garden, drawing on the warmth, airiness and pleasures of the season that prompted people to throw their doors open to the garden. He achieved this through the use of stylised colour artwork which gave a warm, dreamy, glowing quality to the furniture and made it seem a part of the summer. The furniture's placing was deliberately ambiguous: clever use of shadow and perspective made the furniture arranged outside appear as if it were indoors (see page 11); obvious garden features such as flowerbeds were omitted from the artwork. Other advertisements showed the furniture just outside the home, adjacent to the glass doors which were always open, beckoning in the pieces placed outside. The furniture was slowly moving indoors.

SUCCESS IN BRITAIN

The next step in the campaign brought the furniture inside the patio doors. The exterior, again stylised to dreamy effect, lay open to view, with a single table and chair on the patio suggesting possible use in the garden or living room.

As the campaign grew, so did the furniture's popularity, and when it was ordered to furnish British hotels it had at last arrived. When London and North East Railways decided to fill their hotels with Lloyd Loom, it was the seal of approval that Lusty's had been waiting for. In those days, when the railways in Britain were something to be proud of, and station hotels could indeed be regarded as flagships, Lusty's were justified in proclaiming in their full colour advertisements, 'The L.N.E.R. hotels select Lloyd Loom. Follow the leaders!' No respectful middle-class family would want their neighbours to think that they were furnishing their living rooms with garden furniture, but how could it be regarded thus if it furnished respected British hotels? 'The L.N.E.R. experts select genuine Lloyd Loom for furnishing the lounges of their great hotels with charm and dignity. It gives first class service to millions of L.N.E.R. patrons annually.' Out went the stylised artwork; in came photographs showing Lloyd Loom grandly in situ, confirming once and for all that it had come in from the cold. Only occasionally would the furniture be shown in garden settings: the garden door had closed. Henceforth it was respectable living room or bedroom furniture; for that matter, it could be used in the bathroom, nursery, hall, anywhere; even in the garden.

THE L.N.E.R
select

Right: Lusty's 'L.N.E.R. Hotels select . . .' advertisement that marked the success of a four-year campaign to persuade the public to use their furniture in the home and not just the garden (*Ideal Home*, April 1934). All the pieces illustrated, model No. 5294 armchairs and particularly the matching settee, are now rare, collectors' pieces. Some unusual items, also now rare, include a Barbola decorated wastepaper basket, a sewing basket on a stand (with a soft fabric draw-cord top) and a cake stand (almost hidden behind the 'Delux' table).

THREE

MAKING LLOYD LOOM

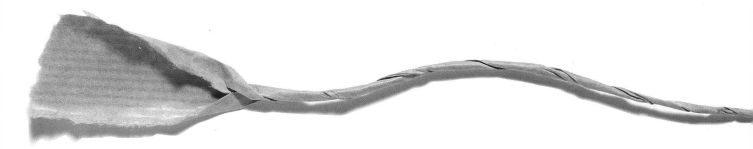

Although Lloyd Loom furniture consisted of fabric that was mechanically woven it would be wrong to assume that the furniture was machine made. The loom was an extremely important part of the process but the woven fibre it provided had to be worked by hand onto frames which were also hand-built. The result was good quality, hand-made furniture, which is why it has survived.

Both Menominee and London factories produced all the components required to make the furniture. Only the very basic materials – rolls of kraft paper, wood and steel – entered their gates. The factories had their own engineers and machine shops for design, maintenance and repair of the equipment. Almost entirely self-sufficient, just about everything, even the manufacture of seating springs, was undertaken inside these factories.

There were four fundamental processes in the production of Lloyd Loom furniture, all of which took place at the factories: framework construction; weaving the fibre on the looms; general assembly of the furniture; and last but

Left: The anteroom to the shower room of the Bath and Racquets Club, Mayfair, London, furnished with Lusty's vintage Lloyd Loom weave pattern chairs (1935–40) and Lusty's table, model No. 8016 (1934–7). Several variations on this table, which has lower shelves suitable for storing books or magazines, were produced in London in the 1930s but they are now difficult to find. *The World of Interiors.* Photograph: James Mortimer.

not least the finishing of the individual pieces. The explanation of each part of the process not only sheds necessary light on the making of the furniture, but also provides details which may be of value and use to the collector of vintage Lloyd Loom.

FRAMEWORK CONSTRUCTION

The majority of vintage (pre-1940) Lloyd Loom used structural frames made from bentwood. In the late 19th century the Austrian Michael Thonet had developed and perfected bentwood dowel furniture. His bentwood chair, made largely from beechwood, was and still is a masterpiece of simplicity. His wood sections were carefully shaped, stained and polished to achieve maximum structural and decorative effect with the minimum materials. His almost skeletal coffee-house style chairs were extremely successful: by 1900 nearly 40,000,000 chairs, made under licence by various manufacturers, had sold worldwide. They were popular in both America and Britain when Lloyd was trying to come to grips with the problems of wicker production.

Perhaps Lloyd was inspired by a Thonet chair. His idea of separating the weave from the frame may have come to him simply by laying his overcoat over a Thonet chair! This possibly whimsical theory has no factual evidence to support it and need not be taken seriously, but it does explain quite visually the production technique adopted by Lloyd. The original, early Lloyd Loom chair is really a bentwood chair covered in Lloyd's woven fibre fabric and bound with fibre so that the bentwood dowel is almost completely hidden. And it is the chair – probably the best known item of Lloyd

Loom – whose manufacturing process will be described in the following pages. The chair was one of the hardest pieces to make.

By the late 1920s the framework had become, in some cases, more complex; not all vintage Lloyd Loom was based on bentwood dowel, but this was Lloyd's original medium and it set the standard from which other variations were derived.

The bentwood manufacturing process was quite straightforward. The hardwood timber was run through machines in the wood mill which stripped and planed sections to size. These were then put into retorts and kept under wet steam pressure for half an hour, to make the wood pliable, before it was put into steel frames that bent and held it to the required shapes. These shapes were set, forming a massive range of structural components that varied from only very slightly shaped leg parts to complex bends and circles,

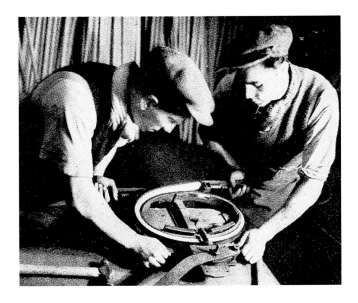

Above: Setting bentwood dowel, made pliable after steaming, into a metal frame. In this case a complete circle, used for a round foot stool or dining chair seat frame, will be formed after the dowel has been thoroughly dried. Lusty's London works, c.1930.

by being placed into large ovens and thoroughly dried. The wooden parts, now permanently shaped, were tested for strength. Defective pieces were discarded. Parts were then stockpiled for the frame makers. There must have been thousands of different dowel lengths, shapes and sizes stocked in this manner for a typical Lloyd Loom chair uses over a dozen different wooden parts, and each chair design would require its own set of parts. To produce a slight variation in the size or shape of an existing design would require a new set of wooden components. Few parts were common to different models, and by the 1930s over 100 different chairs were in production at Lusty's factory in London. Lloyd's introduced new steel tubular legs to some of their furniture designs in 1930. These were produced with a spiral indentation which imitated their traditional fibre-bound dowel and it is, in fact, difficult to differentiate between the two without tapping a coin on, or scratching, their painted surface. These steel legs heralded the beginning of a diversification by Lloyd's into metal furniture production. But the legs, which they initially proclaimed as 'one of the greatest improvements in the manufacturing of woven furniture since the introduction of the famous Lloyd Loom', were not used on all of their designs. In fact they

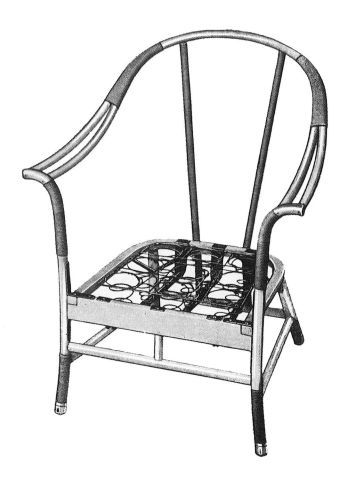

Above: The framework for a Lusty's Delux model No. 60 type armchair, produced from 1924 to 1940 in several size variations. The springs are attached to make a double-sprung cushioned version, but would not be seen if the seat was constructed of woven fibre or used the drop-in 'automobile-type' cushion.

Right: A Lusty's model No. 60 type armchair. c.1928. One of Lusty's 'Delux' chairs which are more easily found nowadays. *Private collection.*

The disappearance of skirts on almost all 1930s American models and on Lusty's 'Popular' range saved labour and therefore reduced production costs, although the savings in material were negligible in comparison. Chairs and settees made without side skirts were easier to construct since the material edge finished on the seat frame (to which it was easily nailed) and this substantially reduced the time spent working the material onto the frame, the most difficult part of the entire manufacturing process.

The material was first applied to the seat section (where this was fibre rather than a sprung cushion). It came pre-cut to fit the exact width of the design which was defined by the metal strips on the edges of both sides which clamped the ends of the filler strands. One edge, that forming the bottom front of the seat section, had its wire stakes plaited back; the other edge, which would be hidden behind the chair back, was rough-cut over size. Chair makers usually specialised in fitting either the seat or the sides/back so that no individual was responsible for the complete construction of the body of a chair or settee. Job rotation was not practised and the craftsmen were paid on a productivity basis so it was in their interests to become highly skilled (and fast) at a single, specialist task.

The seat section was nailed onto the frame at the plaited edge, then pulled firmly through a right-angle over the front of the seat frame and again at its back edge. Several wired stakes were nailed to the underside of the back of the seat frame. When the worker was certain that the material was firm and square it was then nailed though the side metal strips into the seat frame and the back section. Excess fibre was then trimmed. You can see where the stake ends were nailed if you turn a chair upside down. A row of stakes can be seen nailed to the underside back of the chair frame. *This is the hallmark of a genuine early vintage Lloyd Loom.* Most 1930s models have the stake ends covered with a small section of braid to prevent people pricking their fingers whilst lifting chairs by the back edge of the seat.

Not all Lloyd Loom chairs and settees were made with fibre seats. In fact the majority of Lloyd's designs had drop-in upholstered cushions. The early and most expensive designs used cushions with a sprung interior that were laid onto a separate network of springs attached to the framework. These were phased out through the 1920s in favour of an 'automobile'-type drop-in cushion (so called because it was made just like a car seat). All Lloyd's 1930s seating (with the exception of children's chairs) used this system. The cushion was built on a steel chassis that held the coil springs and formed a structure that sat on the seat frame edge and which if removed left a complete void. Lusty's also used both of these systems, the double-sprung as a more expensive optional extra, up to 1940.

Above: Seat cushion springs about to be tempered in an oven. All Lloyd Loom seating springs had an enamel finish baked on to resist rusting. Lusty's factory, c.1933.

Below: A Lloyd Loom interior-sprung cushion used with a separately sprung seat base so that the chair was double-sprung.

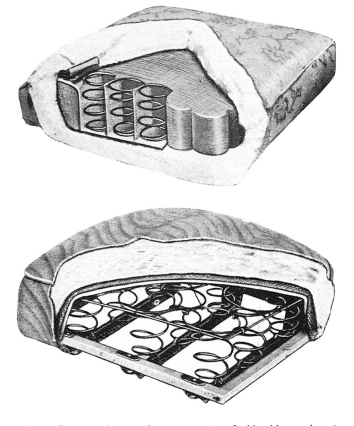

Above: Drawing showing the construction of a Lloyd Loom drop-in 'automobile'-type seat cushion, used on the majority of cushioned chairs made in the 1930s.

Some models were produced both in America and London with permanent upholstery applied to the woven fibre seating back and armrests, but these are now very rare.

The fibre body was applied in the same order of fixing as that of the seat: base-line first (that had been previously plaited-back). The material was then pulled over the inside of the frame's top rail. The worker knelt on the seat and splayed out the loose end of the fabric in order to attain greater flexibility in shaping the material. It was important that all the lines of stakes were parallel and correctly centred to match those of the seat and that they flowed as evenly as possible around the arm shapes which, depending on the complexity of the particular design, might require the material to be stretched or worked rigorously. When the craftsman was satisfied that the material was true it was nailed into place and the excess material carefully trimmed. The decorative braid was then applied both to hide the cut and fixed material edge and to cover the sharp stake ends.

When construction was completed the item was submerged in a weak solution of glue. As this dried, it both sized and tightened the material and structure and acted as an undercoat for the painting process. For items made of dowelling, one last detail required attention (at Lusty's this was done after the painting). All items were levelled on a machine to ensure that they would sit fair and square on the floor. Then, in some of the Menominee models and on all of Lusty's products, the fixing of 'strong solid brass ferrules rung on the legs by patent process' was effected.

These brass feet-caps, or ferrules, are particularly interesting in Lusty's case because they are another good way of differentiating between vintage and post-war products. Almost all Lusty's vintage dowel-leg Lloyd Loom (the majority of their output) was supplied with brass feet-caps. A rubber ferrule was offered as an optional extra but these are rarely seen. Brass ferrules were not standard on Lusty's post-war models. Brass was in short supply after the war and the ferrules were replaced by a domed metal cap which was hammered onto the underside of the end of the dowel leg instead. Towards the end of the 1950s the brass ferrule was again introduced but only as an extra and at an additional cost (also the rubber ferrule) and these are consequently very rarely found on post-war models.

Early Lusty chairs have brass ferrules that were fixed by a simple dot-punch or nail. In the latter part of the 1920s the ferrules were clamped onto the dowel, which produced an indented ring around its circumference. Almost all 1930s models have this indentation marked by serrations caused by the machinery developed for the job. Lloyd's products also had brass ferrule caps, but, as with brass braid caps, their use was inconsistent and they are not a sure guide to the dating of American pieces.

Above: Submerging a chair in a weak solution of glue to size, tighten and provide an undercoat before painting. Lloyd's Menominee factory, c.1927.

Below: A late 1920s brass ferrule used to finish the dowel foot.

Right: A rare Lusty's 1930s cake stand shown in the home of David and Kim Breese; aficionados of Lloyd Loom, they formed Lloyd Loom Furniture Ltd in order to manufacture classic British re-makes (an example of one of these, a dining chair, is shown). Their company has also produced new designs but in a style more reminiscent of the Art Deco period (the settee, coffee and dining table). These have been used to furnish ocean liners, clubs and restaurants in the tradition of British-made Lloyd Loom and Lloyd/Flanders American products.

FINISHING

Lloyd Loom furniture was generally made to order and despatched, finished to customers' particular requirements, within seven days. To be prepared for orders, unpainted furniture was stockpiled and quantities carefully monitored so as to ensure plenty of stock leading up to peak sales' periods. This was explained to the Menominee workers in a November issue of the *Lloyd Shop News*. 'Just now the company is using most of the vacant buildings in the city in order to stock goods. It should be remembered that thousands of dealers do not order their merchandise until they need it. They do not want to or do not have the room and hence wait until spring. Then the orders come in by the thousands and the company cannot keep up with the pace. This means that many car loads [freight train wagons] of merchandise must be manufactured here during the winter so that the spring demands can be met.' The very heavy spring demand was more likely for baby carriages but furniture sales would also have fluctuated through the year. The article was written in 1921, before Lloyd's massive extensions to the Menominee factory were completed. After 1925 there would have been adequate space for storage within the factory.

Lusty's did not have adequate space for storing stock inside their factory so it was kept in a large docklands warehouse about half a mile away. They used special road tractors and trailers to ferry products back and forth between factory and warehouse, which contained between 40,000 and 60,000 pieces of furniture. Lusty's sold directly from stock, so that their customers' orders were swiftly fulfilled. It was also important that items were manufactured in batches of the same design. The 'buffer' stock was necessary as customers' orders might vary from their own production schedule. Thus the road trailers would be fully laden with goods going in both directions: replenishing stocks and taking exact orders to the paint department.

Lloyd's produced hundreds of different items of Lloyd Loom, as did Lusty's, but here there was a crucial difference between the two companies. Lloyd's Menominee factory frequently produced new designs which replaced existing ones. Lusty's also continually developed new designs but kept the majority of their older models and designs in production. The Menominee factory's range of Lloyd Loom furniture therefore never exceeded a hundred items in any single year (substantially fewer during the 1930s), but Lusty's catalogue contained around 400 designs, or design variations, all still in production. (Lloyd's,

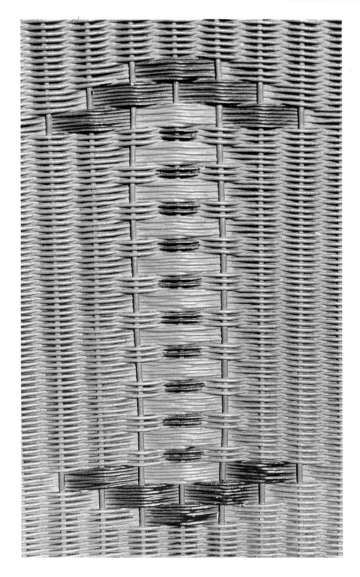

Above: An example of Lloyd's hand-painted pattern weave motif, c.1929. A variety of designs were used, usually to decorate the backs of chairs, and can also be found on Lusty's products.

Left: Spray paint finishing at Lusty's London works, c.1935. The conveyor belt (right) took the newly sprayed items through a tunnel oven (to bake dry the paint) and directly into the packing and despatch department. The photograph shows a diversity of products being finished according to customers' orders. 'Popular' model chairs and linen baskets, items now most easily found, predominate.

it should be remembered, produced a considerable number of baby carriages and diversified into other types of furniture.)

The extent of the furniture range offered by both factories was quite remarkable and it would have been impossible for Lusty's to have kept painted stock of their Lloyd Loom furniture; their colourways alone offered 3000 different options. This meant that they would have had to stock over a million pieces in order to keep just one of each design in each colour. The extraordinary number of colourway options derived from the finishing techniques that they offered. There were eventually thirty-six standard colours available for customers to choose but any of these could be ordered shaded with any of the remaining thirty-five. Shading meant spraying another colour over the base colour to highlight the item's edge or outline. This practice was very popular and is commonly found on vintage pieces which have survived in their original finish.

'Frosted' and 'Misted' colour effects were also offered. Both are interesting because they are sometimes misinterpreted by today's collectors as being unoriginal. Frosted colour was a base colour toned with a contrast colour which was then partly rubbed off, leaving the contrast colour in the hollow of the weave. 'Misted' is also a two-tone colour effect, in this case the base colour was lightly sprayed over with another colour. These finishes were also popular but, to the uninitiated, they may appear as old resprays, a colour applied at a later date and over the original finish (see page 149).

Lusty's also offered 'Double Shading' and 'Misted-Shaded', the latter being a shaded effect softened by being only lightly applied. They also offered a standard 'Oxidised Silver' (silver and black) and 'Oxidised Copper' (copper and black). And, apart from their standard thirty-six colours, their 1930s catalogues noted, 'Should any of these colours be unsuitable for your requirements we can match any special single colour, at the same price as our Frosted effect.' So it is possible to find items of Lloyd Loom furniture in their original colour and in any one of many colours. But that is not all. Lusty's also offered an unpainted option, where the exposed frame (on their 'Popular' models or show-wood 'Delux' models) was stained and polished or left natural and varnished. They also offered other decorative finishes which involved spraying or hand-painting.

Braid and pattern weave motifs could, at an optional and additional cost, be hand-decorated in colours which contrasted with main body colour and highlighted their shapes. These were meticulously picked out with a fine paint brush, a process which was very time-consuming, especially on the braid. Lloyd Loom with its original factory paint finish is now highly prized and especially if this includes hand-painted detail.

In 1934 Lusty's offered a range of stencil patterns that could be 'supplied on any suitable Lloyd Loom model'. These were single colour or two-tone designs of highly stylised forms: flowers, the rising sun, birds and various striped patterns and geometric shapes were the norm. They were too avant-garde for the British taste and did not sell; they were discontinued in 1936 and consequently are rarely found. Children's furniture was also offered in 1934 with optional stencil decoration depicting dogs, cats, ducks and squirrels. These were presumably rather more acceptable and continued to be available, as optional extras, up to 1940.

Perhaps the most bizarre of all of Lusty's special decorations was 'Barbola', three-dimensional shapes that were hand-modelled in clay-like material which set hard onto the loom fabric and was carefully painted 'by [our own] artists, ensuring a delicacy of colouring that is quite unattainable by the use of stencils'.

A special 'art department' was set up in the Lusty factory in about 1930 and it was kept busy applying Barbola to linen baskets, wastepaper baskets and fire screens. This too must have been quite popular because the process remained in production until the factory was destroyed. These, apart from a solitary parrot and a Carolean lady (1938–9) were all floral designs or 'artwork' (they were all individually hand-modelled). Barbola has a certain period charm but the material was so fragile and impractical that one wonders at such a process ever being applied to woven fibre. It was easily cracked or broken and tended to fall off the weave. Barbola is now very rarely found and seldom in perfect condition. A cheaper version of this decorative technique, moulded rather than hand-modelled, was also offered depicting similar forms. Barbola was a rather eccentric British innovation and it was not copied in America. Neither were stencil decorations. But hand-painted decorations to braid and pattern weave motifs *were* more extensively used by Lloyd's, as well as two-tone shading effects, to highlight the more extensive 1930s standard weave patterns.

Left: A Lusty's moulded decoration baked onto the woven fibre and hand-painted. Floral patterns were the most popular.

Right: Lusty's 'Popular' model No. 7064. made between 1933 and 1938. One of a few popular designs made with side skirts and finished with a rare stencil pattern, c.1935. *Collection of the Vitra Design Museum, Weil am Rhein, Germany.*

Lloyd's also offered 'Misted' colour options but limited these to a range of their own choice. Their overall colour range, although excellent, was much smaller than Lusty's and they did not allow the customer the option of specifying colours that were not a part of their own range.

Although such a choice of colour may have excited the public, and although vintage Lloyd Loom can be found in a remarkable number of original colours, the colours most in demand were rather mundane. In my opinion, and based only on the general availability of vintage pieces now found in original colour, the most popular colours appear to have been gold (in Britain) and variations of brown (in America).

The size of Lloyd's spraying operation can be gauged from a quote which appeared in the *Lloyd Shop News* (July, 1920): 'Practically the entire paint department is now in working order on the third floor of the new building . . . Ten sets of drying ovens will be located alongside the sprayers. Each oven will be divided into three compartments, each capable of handling two large trucks of painted articles. By the time the sprayer has filled his third compartment his first would have dried its occupants so that he can fill that again. This will permit a twenty-four hour operation.' But by the late 1920s this system could not cope with the volume required and it was reorganised in favour of an improved conveyor belt-fed oven system. Spray booths were located along breaks in this system so that items could be decorated on a line which led directly to the packing department.

The items were then carefully wrapped, packed and labelled and stacked for delivery. In Menominee a freight train line led directly into the packing department. Lusty's ran several pantechnicons to deliver their goods; bright yellow and proudly displaying their logo, 'Lusty's Lloyd Loom', they would be noticed on roads all over Britain.

Right: A Lloyd/Flanders sofa and table from their 1990 'Classics' range. This furniture is built to last and may easily be confused, in years to come, with vintage models. The latest Menominee factory products are all made with aluminium frames using Lloyd's vintage machinery that rolls flat strips of metal into flawless tubes that cannot rust and, unlike vintage bentwood frame models, are impervious to insect attack. New technology has also enhanced the quality of the woven fibre. This appears identical to the vintage product but is in fact latex-coated and sold with a weatherproof guarantee.

Left: The conveyor belt brings completed products into the packing department. Lusty's London factory, c.1935.

VINTAGE PRODUCTS

Left: Lusty's classic 'Popular' chairs in a garden setting that includes two pattern weave models (1935–40).

Below: 'Popular' chairs furnishing a pub or country hotel interior, c.1936. The tables illustrated are fully bound, 'Delux' models.

WRITING DESKS AND BOOKSHELVES

The huge writing desk seen in Marshal Burns Lloyd's office (page 19) was never put into general production but the smaller model at which Lloyd's secretary is seated was among the items launched to the retail trade by Lloyd's in 1922. The desk top, which had a little wall of woven fibre incorporating two pen pockets at the back, was set onto a pedestal base with short fibre-covered legs. In about 1926 the model was altered, the pedestal ends were rounded and another pen pocket was added to the centre of the back. The model had been discontinued altogether by 1928 but Lloyd's also made another small writing desk in about 1924. This had a shorter fibre body, a lower top wall that did not contain the pen pocket and was in production, with a variation from about 1929, until 1932. The Lloyd Loom writing desk went out of production in America for two years and then an up-dated model, with Jacquard decoration, was made until 1941.

Lusty's copied both of Lloyd's early writing desk designs, discontinuing the longer body version in 1937 and replacing the legs of the other with their cabriole style which continued in production to 1940. All of these Lloyd Loom desks had a small central drawer; American models had

Below: A Lloyd's writing desk, 1924–8, and matching desk chair, c.1928–32. The chair, although suitable for dining, was only promoted as a desk chair by Lloyd's after 1926.

painted or polished wooden tops and the British, as with the majority of their table designs, were all covered with woven fibre and offered with an optional glass cover.

Although Lloyd's own desk was too large to go into production a smaller version of this did appear briefly in America in the early 1920s and in London in about 1927, the latter being named the 'Library Table'. With a large shelf under the top and book shelves at either end of its pedestals, this would have been an ideal, spacious library table. In 1932 the model was redesigned for additional use as a desk and the large lower shelf was partly removed to

Left: Lloyd's 1930s Jacquard decorated writing desk and desk chair (1934–41), with a painted or polished wooden top which, unlike earlier models, was not edged with woven fibre.

provide some leg room. It was made in this form until 1934.

A low bookcase with two shelves large enough to house a set of encyclopaedia was produced by Lusty's from 1931 to 1933, the only Lloyd Loom bookshelf ever made. Writing desks and bookshelves in practically any style or type of manufacture are among the most sought after items of antique furniture and are therefore usually expensive in comparison with other items. One would expect to pay a premium for these. As with most of the items described in the latter part of this chapter, they are now also very rare pieces of Lloyd Loom.

Above: Lusty's versions of the early American Lloyd Loom writing desks made in London, c.1926–37. These were very similar to Lloyd's 1920s desks but were produced with brass castors and fibre-covered tops (with an optional glass cover). The shorter body version (top) was made with polished or painted cabriole legs, 1937–40.

TABLE AND STANDARD LAMPS

Several free-standing table and standard lamps were produced, mostly by Lloyd's. The earliest Lloyd Loom table lamp design, of about 1922, can be seen on the shelf of Lloyd's office couch (page 18). This is made out of sections of sheet fibre set into a painted wooden frame but it is unlikely that this was ever put into production. One of Lloyd's earliest lamps, made in 1923, had a tubular shade of woven fibre with fitch work detail on its lower edge. The flat top was covered with silk on a wire frame which attached the shade to the pedestal. All Lloyd Loom lamps made after 1925 were produced with dome-shaped shades.

Part of Lloyd's patent described the manner in which his woven fibre material could be stretched into oval or rounded shapes by dampening the fibre and applying pressure to the sheet trapped in a mould. The shapes, when submerged in a weak solution of glue, then set firm and retained their shape.

This process was used to produce rounded baby carriage hoods and it was applied in the production of dome-shaped hamper lids and, more extensively, lamp shades and bases. The shade and base were connected by a fibre-bound metal rod or hollowed wooden dowel.

The dome-top table and standard lamp was made in about 1924 and four variations were in production by 1926. Two table lamps were similar but one had a silk-edged fringe on the shade. Both were set on round wooden bases, covered with Lloyd Loom sheet material which was very slightly domed and edged with braid. The two standard lamps had a more pronounced dome-shaped base. One was fitted with a central rod carrying the shade, just as on the table versions, and the other had a decorative polished brass arm, set onto the top of the stand, which held the shade by its top and swung it off centre. This was called the 'Bridge Lamp'.

These early models had an additional bulge on the top of their domed shades which disappeared in 1928 when the range was slightly altered. This alteration took in the need to avoid the woven fibre of the shade being singed by

Above: Lloyd's table lamps as seen in their 1928 trade catalogue. The metal rods that support the shade are less obvious on earlier models which have a bulge at the top of their dome.

the bulb. Metal rods now lifted the shade away from the heat but tended to make the lamps less attractive. The silk fringe option partly covered the support rods on one version but the designs of the other two models, one of which had a square, painted wood base, were greatly compromised. This had an adverse effect on their sales and the table lamp range was completely discontinued by Lloyd's the following year.

The two standard lamp models remained unaltered in production in America until 1931 but for a fancy, turned detail which was added to the base and middle of the column rod in 1928. These were always provided with a silk fringe or, in the case of the Bridge lamp, an optional parchment shade that was 'bought in'; this was the only part of any Lloyd Loom furniture not to be made in their factory.

Lusty's based their three designs for lamps on the American models and they are indeed very similar. An 'Electric Table Lamp' (not all household lamps were electric at this time) was first made in about 1928 and continued in production until 1940. This had a funnel-shaped stand which was hand woven (see Flower Vases, page 111). The earlier models had pull-switches of brass chains, which were discontinued in 1937.

Lusty's standard lamps copied the American Bridge lamp, with a fancy brass adjustable arm holding the shade, and the simpler central column design. But, unlike the American versions, both of these had tripod leg additions set over their dome-shape bases. Lusty's discontinued the Bridge lamp in 1932 but the central column lamp stayed in production along with their table lamp. All of Lusty's three lamp designs were fitted with a silk fringe and they also offered an optional silk lining to the shades. These are now among the rarest items of Lloyd Loom in Europe, especially the bridge and table designs.

Left: Lloyd's 'Bridge Lamp' and an oval table, both c.1929, in a country gazebo, Menominee. This lamp was also originally offered with alternative (non-Lloyd Loom) parchment shades. Lusty's copied the American bridge lamp design in the mid-1920s. It was discontinued by Lloyd's in 1931 and by Lusty's the following year. *Private collection.*

LLOYD LOOM

Left: Lusty's Lloyd Loom table lamp, 21 inches (53cm) high, made with a handwoven base and standard silk fringe, c.1928–40.

Right: Lusty's range of handwoven stands designed for displaying dried flowers and fruit. These unusual items of Lloyd Loom were only in production for a few years in the early 1930s.

Below: An oak panelled living room featuring Lusty's standard lamp, c.1928–40, a cabriole leg coffee table (1935–40) and an occasional table suitable for use as a bookshelf, also produced with a round top (1934–40).

STOOLS

Lloyd's only produced the stool as an upholstered extra for extending lounge chairs into chaise longues, although several models in various sizes were produced in the 1920s to match different chairs. These are all oblong with a squared end that could be pushed up to the chair, the other being rounded. A single model was made in 1929 with a thin, Jacquard decorated band around its body and this continued in production until 1933. No other stools or variations of the stool were produced in America after 1933.

Lusty's had an upholstered chair leg rest similar to the American version (discussed in the Settees section), but they also made several other types of stool. Two base designs used Lloyd Loom seats. The first, a round model, was made in the late 1920s up until 1940. Based on the classic bentwood frame, it was also produced as a dining chair (with a back section added). A tall bar stool version of this model (the only vintage Lloyd Loom bar stool ever made), was produced between 1937 and 1940. The second of Lusty's bentwood framed stools was made between 1932 and 1940. This was oblong with a seat which dipped slightly at its centre. It was also offered with a tubular steel frame from 1937 to 1938.

All the other Lusty's stools (about nine) were of the box and upholstered or cork seat/lid variety and were, in effect, variations of the Lloyd Loom linen basket or ottoman.

Above: Lusty's vintage 'Delux' model dowel frame round stool, 1928–40. This was also made as a (higher) bar stool.

Below: A very rare 1930s Lusty's elongated stool, similar to their stool designed to convert a model type 60 chair into a chaise longue; longer than their production model, it was probably made as a prototype window seat.

FIVE

DATING LLOYD LOOM

For the purpose of dating Lloyd Loom furniture, 1922 was the beginning of it all. That year saw the launch of Lloyd's 'complete line of furniture' in the USA and also the start of Lusty's production in London. Lloyd probably made prototypes of furniture between 1918 and 1920 after he had patented his new system, and would have test-marketed them from 1920 to 1922; any such prototypes – indeed any furniture produced in the early 1920s – is now extremely rare.

Lloyd Loom furniture has been in production for nearly seventy years. It is in mass production again today and, as a revived classic, is likely to remain so for years to come. What is encouraging for collectors of Lloyd Loom is that the vintage furniture can be quite easily and accurately dated. In the case of Lusty's furniture, much of it can be dated to the exact month, even day, of the year it was made. It is even possible to discover the names of the craftsmen responsible for such pieces. This may be common enough in areas of collecting such as silverware and china, but I know of no other 'popular' antique, pre-war furniture where this is possible.

Left: Lloyd's metal trade mark label and card attached to the underside of a standard lamp base, c.1928. Most items of vintage Lloyd Loom produced in the 1920s and '30s by Lloyd's or Lusty's were despatched from the factory with a trade mark label attached, usually hidden on the underside of the item's framework. These often remain intact. *Private collection.*

LABELS, DATE STAMPS AND OTHER MARKS

Almost all genuine Lloyd Loom was originally despatched ex-works with a label attached, either nailed or glued to its frame. The first thing to do in dating a piece is to find its label. On chairs and settees, these are generally attached to the middle of the front seat frame and will be obvious when the piece is turned upside down. Other items, such as linen baskets, lamps and small cabinets, are likely to have labels nailed or glued to the underside of their bases or, with tables, underneath the table top.

Lusty's paid an enormous fee to Lloyd's for the right to produce Lloyd Loom and both they and Lloyd's maintained expensive promotional campaigns. The Lloyd Loom Trade Mark played an important part in their efforts to promote public awareness of their products and to protect copyright. In America a black and silver metal tag was first used, later followed by a gold foil transfer.

Lusty's preferred to use a card label and in some cases a celluloid tag. To drive the message home they tied a separate, octagonal card tag to every item that left their factory just to inform the public that their trade mark was 'permanently attached elsewhere on every article of Lloyd Loom models made by W. Lusty & Sons Ltd'. These tags are now extremely rare because they were meant to be discarded by the purchaser before the item was put into use, but because the other labels were firmly attached to the framework they are often found intact. In Lusty's case these can make the precise dating of the furniture extremely simple. Lusty's frequently altered the style of their labels producing eighteen different designs or variations pre-war and, from 1930 on, stamped a date onto the furniture frame. Such date stamps can be misleading, as will be explained later, but in many instances items of British-made Lloyd Loom can be very simply dated by their original label or stamp mark.

It is sometimes possible to discern another stamp on the underside of Lusty's wooden framework which has nothing to do with dating; this was the 'signature' of the craftsman responsible for constructing the item or those responsible for quality control checks. Where signatures do exist on vintage furniture they are usually hidden under the paint finish, and are therefore only visible on items still in their original unpainted finish, which would have been a light stain or varnish. (See illustration, page 134.)

Lloyd's, unfortunately, did not apply date stamps to their furniture and used only two different trade mark label designs from 1922 to 1941. To comply with state laws concerning the use of materials other labels were also applied. Although labels do not help to date American Lloyd Loom as accurately as they do British, they are nevertheless a boon to collectors and help to differentiate between early pieces and later vintage models.

Above: Lloyd's 1920s black on silver/metal trade mark label, found nailed to framework. Shown approximately full size.

LLOYD'S: LABELS

Lloyd's earliest furniture trade mark label was stamped out of metal and over-printed black as a negative, so that the lettering was metallic (silver) rather than a printed colour. Such labels were nailed onto the frame and generally seem to have stayed there, neither falling off in the intervening years nor suffering any significant damage. (The label can be cleaned if it has been over-painted and in most cases the original lettering will remain legible.) This label was phased out in the later 1920s and can be used to identify Lloyd's early models. It is rarely found on furniture produced after 1929.

None of Lloyd's trade mark labels contains any reference to Heywood-Wakefield and it is sometimes mistakenly assumed that this dates them to before 1921 (the year Heywood-Wakefield purchased Lloyd's). The labels are all marked 'Method Patented Oct, 16, 1917', so it is easy to understand this mistake if one follows the reasoning that furniture production begun in 1917 and that the label would have carried the name 'Heywood-Wakefield' after 1921. But this is not what happened.

A label which carried the name did so to comply with the legislation of several states concerning 'sanitary bedding laws and laws regulating the manufacture and sale of upholstered furniture'. In order to comply, items of furniture required a label to be fixed to them which, 'under penalty of law', could not be removed. This noted that the item was made with 'all new material'. Most of Lloyd's seating was made with soft fabric cushions but even lamps, which used silk lining, were required to carry the label. These were printed on card which was stapled onto the furniture frame, usually alongside the trade mark label, but, being card, they were more likely to be lost or damaged.

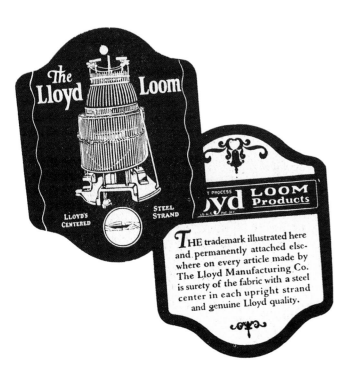

Above: Facsimile of Lloyd's 1920s tie-on card tag. Designed to inform the public that the Lloyd Loom trade mark was 'permanently attached elsewhere on every article made by The Lloyd Manufacturing Co.'

Left: An early Lloyd's 'sanitary law' card label, c.1925. *Collection of Bob and Dina Meissner, Menominee, MI, USA.*

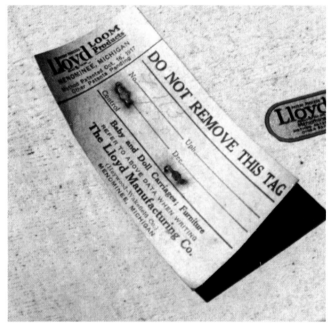

On these 'Heywood-Wakefield' appears in small lettering in brackets under 'Lloyd Manufacturing Co'. This label was also applied to baby carriages and where these pre-date 1921 'Heywood-Wakefield' is not mentioned. It is therefore possible that furniture labelled in this way is also pre-1921, although this will be extremely rare.

Lloyd's 'sanitary law' label altered its design and although this has not been fully researched it appears that one of the earliest of these (applied to furniture) depicted Lloyd's head in a small oval captioned 'Inventor'. A label of about 1927 copied the metal trade mark 'Lloyd Loom products' logo and included 'furniture and baby carriages', which was printed vertically, to the side of the main text. Post-1928 labels appear similar but replace the vertically printed 'furniture and baby carriages' with the company address and patent information.

In about 1928 Lloyd introduced a new trade mark which was applied to furniture as a transfer; it was made out of a fine gold coloured metallic foil with black lettering and a red border. This was used until 1941 and although it cannot 'fall off' the furniture, being a flat transfer, it is harder to find if heavily over-painted.

Above right: A Lloyd's 'sanitary law' card label, c.1929.

Right: Lloyd's red and gold trade mark label, c.1929. This was a fine transfer, glued to the frame, that succeeded the nailed silver/metal label and was used on most furniture made in the 1930s. Shown approximately full size.

Above: Lusty's octagonal trade mark tie-on tag. Designed for the same purpose as Lloyd's example – to inform the public (on its reverse side) that another trade mark was 'permanently attached elsewhere'.

LUSTY'S: LABELS AND DATE STAMPS

Lusty's used several different label designs in the 1920s and 1930s. Date stamps first appeared in 1930 and for a short time were placed to one side of their trade mark label. Early date marks gave the exact day, month and year of each item immediately before it was despatched from the factory, but the majority indicate the month and year in abbreviated form: DEC 32, SEP 36, etc. These were hidden under the trade mark label. Date stamps were applied, and hidden under the label, as a way of assessing the durability of their products and as part of their quality control system, which Lusty's always applied fastidiously. A catalogue of Lusty's labels and the date stamps associated with these follows and provides the reader with an extremely simple and accurate method of dating. But Lusty's labels and date stamps can, in some cases, be misleading.

The problem here arises because of the 're-enamelling and renovation' service Lusty's offered their customers. This was used not only as a 'service to make worn or damaged furniture as good as new' but also in cases where customers simply wished to change their interior colour scheme. The service was well subscribed. Lusty's did not apply their labels and date stamps for the benefit of future generations of collectors; once again, they were but a part of quality control. When an item of furniture was finished, and regardless of its original date of manufacture, a new label was always added with a stamp to indicate the date of the renovation.

Right: An early Lusty's date stamp, May 1930. Date stamps were first applied to furniture in this year adjacent to the trade mark labels.

Left: A rare Lusty's 'Delux' model No. 85 armchair (1926–40). *Private collection.*

I have seen many instances of original 1920s and thirties furniture with post-war labels and date stamps. Although these are quite obviously incongruous, the system was in operation from the late 1920s and pre-war refurbishments are not so obvious. But Lusty's help us out here because they stamped the letter 'R' onto the frame, either to one side of or over the newly applied label. This has sometimes been misinterpreted as 'R' for 'reject', which is not the case. Beware of the letter 'R' when assessing age by labels and date stamps.

Above: Example of a label and date stamp (under the label) that can confuse dating. Lusty's 'R' for 'refurbishment' is, in this case, clearly stamped over the label but it is often found on the frame adjacent to the label and sometimes faded and less obvious. The label was applied in the late 1930s but it is attached to a very early table (c.1922) with legs covered in wired woven fibre rather than binding.

Lusty's rejects in fact provide us with the biggest problem with regard to labels and date stamps, not because they were stamped with misleading marks, but because they carried no marks or labels whatsoever! A Lusty's reject would only be – because of tight quality control – a very marginal 'second best', and this perhaps only in the paint finish. It would be impossible now to differentiate between rejects and those pieces which have faded and taken on the patina of age (now highly prized!). But items do exist which were never labelled or dated, and this is probably because they were purchased directly by Lusty's staff, as seconds, along with prototype models. There was a waiting list for the staff purchase of such items and, as Lusty's employed several hundred people and produced millions of pieces of furniture, items with neither labels nor date stamps are by no means rare.

But in cases where the label has been lost or the date stamp over-painted by some fastidious decorator (not at all uncommon) some information on dating can still be gleaned. If the date stamp is visible, you have your exact date of manufacture and can at least find out which label you are missing using the catalogue of label designs. If the label is missing and you cannot find a date stamp, look for the protruding nail heads in the framework which would have held the card in place. If these are apparent, the item is pre-1930 rather than a 'second' or prototype, which could be of any date.

If the label has been been completely painted over, although it will be illegible at least it has been protected and will eventually give up its information. And remember, in the majority of cases no date stamp means a pre-1930 piece. If the label is missing and the frame has been painted over you can detect whether the item is pre- or post-1931 by measuring the space between the nail heads. The catalogue of labels reproduces the labels to actual size for this reason; you may notice that there is a distinct difference between the sizes of pre- and post-1930 labels. The nail head spacings will match one or the other. If the space between nail heads is the wider of the two, the date stamp will be under the paint between the nail heads or, perhaps, in a few cases (1930–31), adjacent to them. Enthusiasts have been known to strip off the paint to find dates and if you are so inclined this can be done. The shorter space between nail heads will tell you that the model is pre-1931 and any further digging around will be unnecessary.

Date stamps and labels were always applied after the final paint finish, which was, as you may remember from the chapter on making the furniture, not necessarily the date when the furniture was manufactured. Lusty's fulfilled orders from their stock warehouse which were then brought back to the factory for painting. This warehouse contained around about 50,000 pieces. It is not therefore impossible to find an item which was actually produced some years earlier than the date which it was finally painted. Unlike Lloyd's in Menominee, Lusty's kept certain designs in production over many years; I have noticed items with original labels and date stamps which, for a variety of reasons – method of construction, date of discontinuation etc – could not have been produced in the year they were stamped.

Right: Lusty's 'Delux' model No. 53 armchair (1922–40). The example shown was made in the late 1920s but returned to the factory for a respray in the 1950s and has a misleading 1950s label and date stamp on its seat frame. *Private collection.*

LUSTY'S POST-WAR LABELS (all actual size)

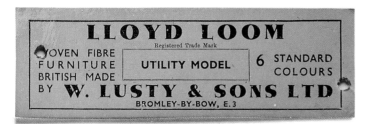

LLOYD LOOM
Registered Trade Mark
WOVEN FIBRE FURNITURE BRITISH MADE BY | UTILITY MODEL | 6 STANDARD COLOURS
W. LUSTY & SONS LTD
BROMLEY-BY-BOW, E.3

Nos 19 and 20. Card labels, c.1945–50. Date stamp beneath label and/or utility stamp adjacent to label.

Above: The utility logo and (right) how it appears stamped on the frame.

No.21. 1950s card label. Date stamp beneath card.

No.22. 1950s celluloid label.

No.23. 1960s plastic label or similar design on metallic foil.

Nineteen-fifties labels (Label Cat. Nos 21 and 22) are the most simplistic of all Lusty's Lloyd Loom label designs and are instantly recognisable by their use of the freehand-style 'Lusty' logo, which had been used by Lusty's on their vintage advertisements, shop display materials and octagonal tie-on tags. This label is sometimes found on earlier, pre-war furniture sent back to Lusty's for repainting or renovation in the fifties.

The rebuilt Lusty Bromley-by-Bow factory complex finally closed in 1963 and all production moved to Martley. The 1960s label was renewed along with the style of furniture the company produced and appears as an oval plastic tag, usually stapled onto the framework or as a metallic foil transfer.

Above: Colour artwork for a Lusty's magazine advertisement, c.1957. The dressing table stool illustrated uses tapered dowel legs typical of the period. The linen basket retains the 1930s look but was made with a hardboard (rather than a solid wooden plank) base.

Right: A stylish contemporary 1950s Lusty's chair on a tubular steel frame. This model was made with a weave variation, sometimes found on post-war models which, although similar to vintage Jacquard decoration, was woven as a uniform sheet. *Collection of the Vitra Design Museum, Weil am Rhein, Germany.*

Woven Fibre Density (page 51)

The spacing between the wired stakes in the weave changed in 1931 from 1 inch to ¾ inch (25mm to 19mm). Some items c.1931 can be found with both types of weave density. All items with ¾ inch weave are products of the 1930s but the wider weave can be found on some American models produced through the thirties and on some of Lusty's models made until 1934.

Jacquard Decorated Woven Fibre (page 51)

A change in uniformity of the weave that created a contrast in the pattern of the woven fibre; used as a decorative technique it was often highlighted by original paint finish. Small geometric motifs, often centred on chair backs, are usually found on 1920s products.

Extensive Jacquard decoration appeared only after 1930. This is found on most 1930s American products, but rarely on Lusty's products until 1935 and then only on their range of 'Popular' chairs, made until 1940.

Fitch Work (page 87)

Areas of open weave where filler strands are not used and the wired stakes were used to decorative effect. Fitch work appeared on some American products from 1922 to 1932 and on only very few British products 1930 to 1933. Now very rare.

Stick Fibre (page 87)

Furniture constructed using only wired stakes. Stick fibre was used in American products from 1928 to 1931, in British only about 1931. Now extremely rare.

Show-Wood Frames (page 78)

Items made using turned/carved and polished wood as decorative framework. American products 1929–31. British models, 1929–37.

Cabriole Legs (page 78)

Polished or painted wooden 'Queen Anne' or cabriole-style legs. British-made products only, 1935–40.

Square Wooden Framework (page 79)

Models with square wooden legs and framework that was not bound with fibre. British models only, 1933–40.

Metal Lookalike Framework (page 48)

Painted tubular steel framework or part frame (legs) which looks very similar to fibre bound dowel. American products only, 1930–35.

Tubular Steel Framework (page 81)

Painted or chromium plated tubular steel frames. American products, 1931–33. British models, 1935–40.

Flat-Section Steel Cantilevers (page 82)

Painted or chromium plated flat-section steel cantilever chair bases. American products 1931–41. British models, 1933–40.

Below: A Lusty's late 1950s armchair with the traditional woven fibre body shape subtly modernised. This model, as with that shown on page 137, illustrates Lusty's 1950s tubular steel frame which was much thinner than those used pre-war.

Left: A Lusty's model U64 armchair produced after 1945. It was enormously successful and consequently is not difficult to find. The example depicted is, however, unusual for its Jacquard decoration, rarely found on Lusty's post-war products; this example may have been a one off. The chair does, however, lack two fundamental features, which marks it as a post-1945 Lusty's product – binding on the framework and brass feet caps. *Author's collection.*

SIX

CARE, REPAIR AND ASSESSING VALUE

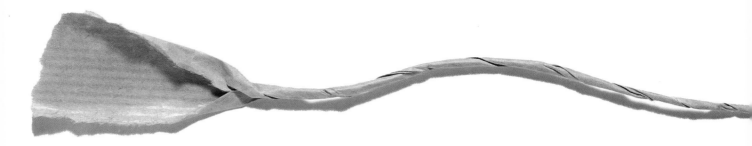

Vintage Lloyd Loom furniture can be found in excellent and original condition but there are pitfalls that one should be aware of when buying this furniture. As with any other antique collecting one should always try to buy the best. The condition of a piece is obviously important to its value, perhaps more so in the case of Lloyd Loom than with most other types of furniture because the woven fibre is often an integral part of the structure and its final finish. The linear pattern inherent in the weave is crucial to the aesthetic, as becomes clear when it is spoilt by a poor attempt at repainting or repair. But damage can be repaired or, better still, avoided.

INSECT ATTACK

Although Lusty's proclaimed in their early advertisements that Lloyd Loom was 'impervious to insect attack', it is as well to examine the wooden framework carefully. The woven fibre evidently provides a miserable meal for woodworm, but the hardwood dowel is susceptible to insect attack and it is easy to overlook this. Inspect the frame for woodworm bore holes, especially around structural joints. Woodworm can be quite easily treated using a

Left: A very rare Lusty's armchair, c.1922. One of their earliest chairs and probably a prototype for model No. 28 (page 138). This example uses split cane binding, found only on Lusty's earliest chairs. The woven fibre on its armrests has been damaged but these holes can be quite easily repaired.

proprietary fluid available from hardware stores. Do not be unduly concerned if the odd hole is discovered; once treated, an item is unlikely to have suffered much structural damage. But one should think twice before investing in an item of Lloyd Loom which is truly riddled with worm. If the frame snaps because of this, the entire piece could be a write-off. It can be difficult to spot infestation when the framework is fully bound with fibre twine but bore holes and powder residue will be evident and the structure may be rickety. So do not forget to check this.

DAMAGE TO THE WEAVE AND FRAMEWORK

The only place where Lloyd Loom material is likely to wear is the front edge of woven fibre seats, where the woven fibre is turned through a right angle over the seat frame. Chairs and settees are both susceptible to heavy wear but in general illustrate well the remarkable strength of Lloyd Loom. It is unlikely that you will find many vintage models with badly worn weave on their arms, backs or anywhere on the body, despite constant use. The same applies to old woven seats; most are in excellent condition, the fibre seldom worn out. But chairs with woven fibre seats do have a problem inherent in their structural design. Always inspect the area of the weave along the front edge of an easy chair or settee because it is common to find that the woven fibre has sagged immediately below the point where it is supported by the frame. The extent to which the material has stretched and sagged will depend on how heavily the item has been used; if excessively, the outline of the underlying frame edge will be noticed. In this case one should examine the wired stakes for breaks as they are now, in effect, being worked onto a sharp edge each time the seat is used. This will eventually lead to the seat splitting along the front edge. The problem, of course, does not occur where seating was made with sprung cushions but vintage items with woven fibre seats can often be ruined as a result of this damage.

Any other breaks found in Lloyd Loom weave are likely to have been caused by accidental damage, usually to items poorly protected in transit. It is possible to do more harm to an item of Lloyd Loom simply by driving it around the block, unprotected in the back of a van, than it may have suffered from fifty years of general use. Take as much care with Lloyd Loom as you would with any other polished or panelled antique. Lloyd Loom looks, and is, remarkably resilient but if the woven fibre is badly scratched or punctured it is difficult to repair. Be protective when moving Lloyd Loom from one place to another; it should be wrapped in a blanket, well secured and kept away from sharp or pointed objects.

The framework generally suffers from worm infestation rather than accidental damage because the hardwood dowel is incredibly strong. It can, however, become loose at the joints or warp and this is often the case with vintage items which have been left outside for a long time. In such cases the fibre may also have lost its protective finish and rotted, or the wires in the stakes rusted and therefore substantially weakened. Beware of any items that appear to have 'furry' fibre, are a washed out grey colour or have hairline cracks in the dowel. These are usually the signs of a very sick piece of Lloyd Loom, one that has either been dipped in a stripping tank or retrieved from some forgotten corner of the garden. Such an item is unlikely to be a good, functional piece of furniture and may, unless it is very rare, turn out to be a pointless investment. But apart from these extreme cases most damage can be repaired and, if treated with respect, this furniture will survive many years of use.

SMALL WEAVE REPAIRS

It takes quite a hefty, sharp blow to damage the wired stakes in the body of the weave but the filler strands woven about these are more easily snapped. The odd broken filler strand may be found practically anywhere in the weave and, although these will not harm the strength of the item's overall structure, they should be repaired. Loose, broken ends may eventually fray or get caught and snap back to the nearest stake, leaving a small but noticeable gap in the weave.

The best glue to use when repairing woven fibre is the modern PVA woodworking variety. This is transparent when dry, strong and, unlike many other types of glue,

excess quantities or mistakes can be wiped away (before dry) with a damp cloth. A tiny spot applied to each broken end should suffice and the fibre should be held in place, while the glue dries, using a low-tack masking tape.

Repairing small holes in the woven fibre is not too difficult where the wired stakes are still intact, as is often the case. The immediate problem here is the need for replacement material. This is available and is listed together with specialist restorers, manufacturers of contemporary Lloyd Loom and other useful contacts on page 160. The process of repairing a hole in the woven fibre is illustrated (right) in eight simple stages. (One of the arm sections of the chair shown on page 142.)

1. The woven fibre has been punctured and some of the filler strands lost or damaged so that they cannot be rejoined.
2. Start the repair by snipping back all the broken filler strands to the nearest wired stake.
3. Space has now been created for the new filler strands and the loose or frayed ends of any old strands have been removed.
4. Cut a new length of fibre slightly longer than needed. Apply glue to one end and tuck this firmly into the weave so that it overlaps the end of the original strand. Work on the face which is most commonly viewed. In many cases, such as the example illustrated, the reverse side of the repair will be hidden and any overlapping strands will not be noticed so no attention need be given to the back of the repair. Where a repair is likely to be viewed from both sides overlapping fibre may be noticed so greater care will be required in joining the new fibre to the original.
5. Thread the new fibre along its course, snip to size, apply glue and tuck the end into position. The new strand should now lie snugly against the existing fibre.
6. Continue the process.
7. You may need to adjust the alignment of the new fibres after each new length is fitted.
8. When all the new fibres are in position the repair will still be flimsy. Glue has so far only been applied in order to tack down the fibre ends but when the patch is sealed the repair will become solid. It should be sealed with a mixture of the suggested glue and water (50:50) which can be brushed over the repair and will seep down into the weave. This also acts as a primer for the paint finish which shall also help to mask and bind the new patch (see page 146).

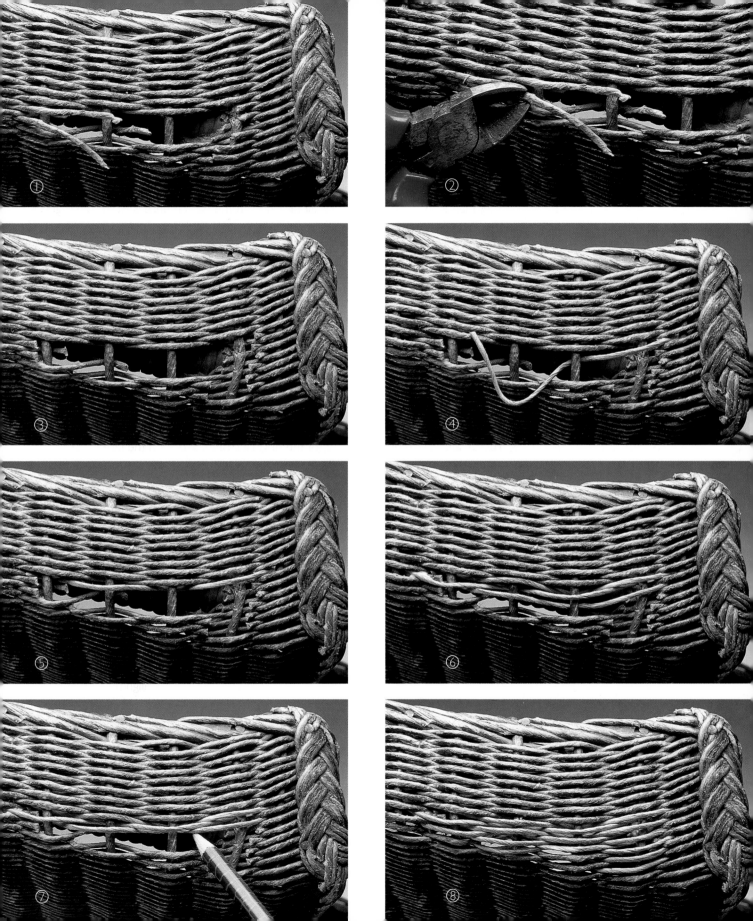

Left: Searching for vintage Lloyd Loom. Six woven fibre chairs can be seen in this photograph (taken in an antiques warehouse in Bermondsey, London). One of the six chairs is a Lloyd Loom lookalike, the others are original Lusty's models ranging in date from c.1923 to 1956. *(Left to right)* a mid-1930s weave pattern 'Popular' model. The gold colour looks remarkably fresh and on close examination a 1950s Lusty's label and 'R' stamp were found attached to the chair, verifying the fact that it had been resprayed by Lusty's in the 1950s; a rare square-backed armchair, c.1923 and instantly recognisable as an early chair by its separated skirt. This model, with its unusual open arm design, went out of production in 1933 and represents an exceptionally lucky find; *(above this chair, in background)* a 1950s Lusty's armchair in its original green colour and in a style based on their 1930s 'Popular' designs. On close examination the chair is found to have been made without any binding or brass ferrules and with tubular steel leg stretchers, a product of the 1950s and clearly labelled as such; a 1930s square backed armchair with a cushioned seat. This model is difficult to find but the example shown has been spoilt by being heavily over-painted; a Lloyd Loom lookalike over-painted in white, made from woven fibre but without wired stakes; such models lack the resilience of Lloyd Loom and comparatively few have survived; a 1940s Lusty's U64 model which, although in its original light green colour, is in poor condition and requires restoration.

HOW MUCH IS IT WORTH?

Vintage Lloyd Loom has only recently come to be regarded as 'antique', and some vintage models have achieved a new status as twentieth-century design classics. This has influenced modern furniture manufacturers. Some of the old designs are being copied and there is a large market for new Lloyd Loom made in the traditional style. Lloyd Loom is not easily reproduced. New products based on classic designs usually cost more than originals selling in antique shops. Vintage Lloyd Loom was never cheap; it was reasonably priced furniture which represented good value for money. In the mid-1930s the majority of Lusty's 'Delux' chairs retailed at between £2 and £3, an apparently ludicrous price but relative, of course, to the typical wage of the period. A skilled craftsman working a forty-eight hour week in Lusty's factory in London would not have taken home more in his pay packets than this, the average price of a good quality Lloyd Loom chair. Lusty's employees were not underpaid and nor were Lloyd's where a similar comparison can be made. Put into this context, many items of old Lloyd Loom furniture are presently less expensive than they were before the war.

One does not need, therefore, to be particularly wealthy in order to purchase an excellent example of original vintage Lloyd Loom; it compares very favourably with

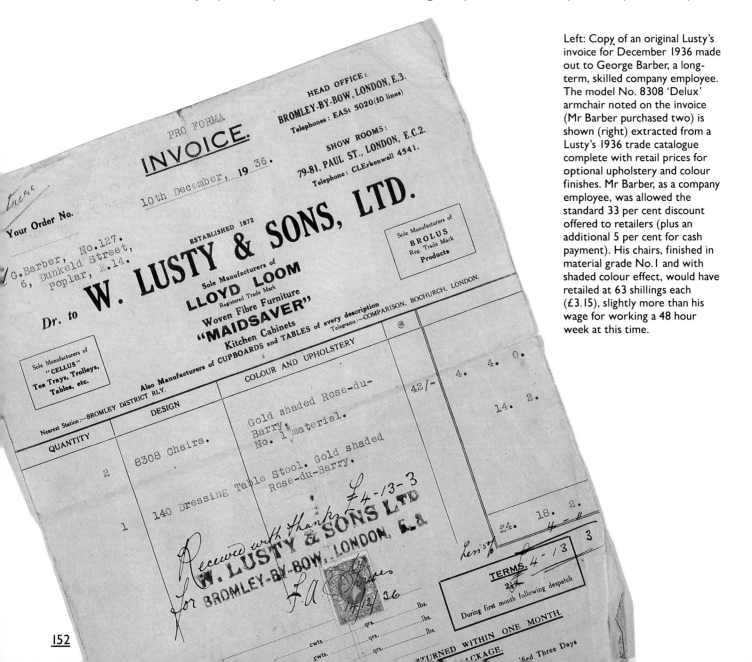

Left: Copy of an original Lusty's invoice for December 1936 made out to George Barber, a long-term, skilled company employee. The model No. 8308 'Delux' armchair noted on the invoice (Mr Barber purchased two) is shown (right) extracted from a Lusty's 1936 trade catalogue complete with retail prices for optional upholstery and colour finishes. Mr Barber, as a company employee, was allowed the standard 33 per cent discount offered to retailers (plus an additional 5 per cent for cash payment). His chairs, finished in material grade No. 1 and with shaded colour effect, would have retailed at 63 shillings each (£3.15), slightly more than his wage for working a 48 hour week at this time.

many other types of antique furniture in terms of value for money. It has increased in value quite dramatically in the last few years but it is still relatively inexpensive and its value is likely to continue to rise.

Currently, the most valued items of vintage Lloyd Loom are settees and larger chairs but these are still not expensive in relation to other forms of seating. It is difficult to find large chairs and settees of antique character which are comfortable, practical and versatile in that they can harmonise with a variety of different interior decor schemes. Antique living room furniture tends to be heavily upholstered; purchase price apart, the cost of upholstering it to one's individual taste will usually exceed the price

asked for an excellent vintage Lloyd Loom model, which generally will not require expensive new upholstery.

Lloyd Loom is becoming 'collectable'. Many hundreds of thousands of items of vintage Lloyd Loom exist and it is possible to find early, unusual or very rare items selling alongside the more commonplace pieces without any price differentiation. If this situation continues, and individuals' knowledge of the subject develops, Lloyd Loom collecting will differ from almost every other established field of collecting. Items known to be rare, unusual or significant to the history of a popular subject are usually valued at a premium. In this case, Lloyd Loom is popular but very little is as yet known about it. It has the potential to develop into a fascinating and rewarding field for the collector, investor or anyone who simply wishes to purchase some useful and interesting furniture.

It would be unrealistic to list the value of items of Lloyd Loom in the manner of an 'antiques price guide' as prices for vintage Lloyd Loom are still topsy-turvy. At the time of writing, there is no established consensus of opinion in the American or European antiques trade that would make this task viable. Apart from large chairs and settees which have established premium prices simply by virtue of being large, most other items dating from the 1920s to the 1950s are sold simply as 'old Lloyd Loom'. And because there are so many different types and styles of vintage Lloyd Loom, and thus scope for different opinions, any valuation of individual items by this writer would be purely subjective. But having said that, it is possible to identify those aspects which affect saleability and to provide the reader with a system which will assist in valuation and also give tips on how best to buy or sell Lloyd Loom furniture.

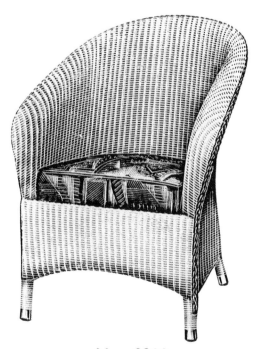

No. 8308
Height 32 in.   Width 27 in.
Single Sprung (Auto Construction) Seat.
18 in. × 18 in. × 18 in. High.

Material	X or Duck	1	2	3
STANDARD COLOURS	55/6	60/-	64/6	67/6

No. 8208
Spiral Spring Seat and Spring Cushion.

STANDARD COLOURS	63/-	67/6	72/-	75/-

Shaded, Misted or Frosted Effects, 3/- extra cost.

ASSESSING VALUE

The value of any individual piece of Lloyd Loom will depend on its condition, rarity and popularity. The items which score most favourably on all these counts will represent the most sought after and potentially most valuable pieces. The importance of these three factors is discussed, followed by a points system which can be used to assess the value of any individual item.

Condition is not too difficult to assess as far as outright damage is concerned. The best pieces should neither be damaged nor worn and there is plenty of vintage Lloyd Loom around which, if repainted, would look brand new. This represents the best possible condition and can be found, even where items date from 1922. Do not assume that any early piece of vintage Lloyd Loom will be shabby because of its age.

The material itself (the structure) need not necessarily be worn at all, but its colour or finish should appear mellow and faded with age. There is here an apparent contradiction: an undamaged item becomes 'damaged' if it is newly painted.

Vintage items which appear to be brand new (i.e. they have been newly painted) are generally less valuable than those which show their age. This is important to the extent that a well-worn item, with small weave breaks but in its original colour, will be more valuable than the same item in immaculate condition but newly painted.

An item which is extensively damaged may require specialist restoration and this may exceed the cost of a similar item in perfect condition. So, unless the item is extremely rare, or is valued for personal reasons, it may presently have very little value. Note the word 'presently': it is relevant because certain items of Lloyd Loom may eventually merit restoration. A Lloyd Loom settee with a broken seat that was considered worthless and thrown out a few years ago might now be valuable and well worth the cost of extensive restoration.

As this is the first book to explain and illustrate the range of Lloyd Loom furniture, its rarity value is as yet little understood. This book identifies many items which are now exceptionally difficult to find. Collectors may never have a second chance to buy a particularly rare item and this may affect valuation of such an item, purely in practical terms. Sellers of vintage Lloyd Loom may adjust their prices for rare items to take account of this fact. In this way rarity affects prices but this is relative to knowledge and interest in the subject.

Rarity is also relative to geographical location. American Lloyd Loom is currently very rare in Europe but it is probable that many of Lusty's old pieces have been shipped to the United States as Britain has a well-established export market for its old furniture. This situation may change, Lloyd's old products may be shipped to Europe, but this would not cause the European market to be flooded with the chairs pictured in Marshall Burns Lloyd's office! Products dating from the 1920s are generally difficult to find, although this is less true of American Lloyd Loom than that produced in Britain. Lloyd's actually produced more Lloyd Loom in the 1920s than they did in the 1930s and the reverse is true for Lusty's.

Popularity is to do with current fashion which, as everyone knows, is fickle. Lusty's offered cabriole legs on many of their models in the mid-1930s because the style was in vogue at the time. Interestingly, none of the manufacturers of contemporary Lloyd Loom has chosen to offer a cabriole leg option. The items which are likely to be least affected by future fashion trends are those which are deemed to be classics, items which epitomise the best of the vintage period. Popularity is also influenced by practicality: furniture is usually required to be functional. Lloyd Loom is generally well suited to life in the 1990s although some pieces are more useful than others. Coffee tables immediately spring to mind. These were much less popular in the 1920s than today, which is unfortunate because they are now much sought after but very difficult to find. The same is true of children's furniture. Large chairs and settees are now very popular as good, practical furniture but they are hard to find. Too big to store away when they went out of fashion, they suffered the same fate as so much other Lloyd Loom. And there are many items of Lloyd Loom that are becoming popular with specialist collectors because they are unusual and, as these were produced in relatively small quantity, are difficult to find.

In the points system established to evaluate the best quality Lloyd Loom – the pieces likely to command a high price – a worthwhile investment will score eight points or more out of a possible twelve.

CONDITION

Immaculate condition and original paint ****
Some wear but original paint ***
Immaculate but newly painted **
Some wear and newly painted *

NB Count nothing for items with weave clogged by repainting or damage that requires restoration.

RARITY

Rare ****
Any product of the 1920s ***
Any product of the 1930s *

POPULARITY

Settees and large chairs ****
Children's furniture ****
Coffee tables ****
All other items ***

NB Subtract one point for items with cabriole or steel cantilever legs where these were optional. Add a point for items with fitch work detail.

Right: A rare Lusty's 'Delux' model No. 66 armchair with a rounded front skirt, c.1930 (produced 1928–33). Immaculate in its original dark Jacobean frosted gold colour and worthy of twelve points on the quality scale. *Collection of the Anacara Company, Stamford, CT, USA.*

This points system balances condition against rarity and popularity to illustrate how these factors have an effect on value. The Popularity section does not list all the various types of Lloyd Loom because it relates to Rarity in this respect. For example, Lloyd Loom table lamps or desks are very popular with specialist collectors but are also rare and will therefore score eight points even if worn and newly painted. A small easy chair made in the 1930s is easy to find by comparison but will only score eight points if it is in immaculate and original condition. A large chair or settee, children's furniture or a coffee table may score eight points, even if restoration is required as these are both rare and popular with a larger market.

BUYING OR SELLING – SOME TIPS

In both Europe and America antique shops, auctions and antique markets are obviously the best places for both buying and selling old Lloyd Loom, but be prepared for a wide variety of prices. The market for any item of old furniture is inconsistent. Markets differ between countries and even in different areas within the same town and there is no standard price list for vintage Lloyd Loom.

You should pay whatever you believe to be reasonable and affordable, and you can value individual items of Lloyd Loom quite simply by comparing them with other types of furniture, old or new, available locally. There need be no mystery in assessing if this furniture represents good value for money as useful, practical furniture.

The trouble with buying any old item of furniture is that if you are in effect 'going fishing', each piece will be by virtue of its personal history, age, and condition, unique. If you find an item that you like and can afford, buy it. Vintage Lloyd Loom is not re-orderable. If you think you can buy a piece cheaper elsewhere at least try to reserve the item while you look around. Most antiques dealers will accommodate you in this respect. It can be extremely disheartening to return to find that the item you were interested in has been sold. If you wish to sell an item of Lloyd Loom to the antique trade do not expect a dealer to make a trip to your home in order to give you a free valuation. Some may be prepared to do this, but most dealers will want to know your price. If you are unclear about its value, go around as many antique shops as you can manage with a good, clear photograph of the item you want to sell. A dealer will tell you what he is willing to pay and you can consider the offers made to you at leisure.

Auctions can be useful either for buying or selling vintage Lloyd Loom. Terms and conditions of sale and purchase vary from place to place but, in most cases, auctioneers' charges will effect the amount you receive, so study their terms. If you are buying always carefully inspect the item during the auction preview. Mark your bid to account for any charges which may be imposed over the hammer price. Decide the absolute maximum that you are prepared to pay for the item and stick to this. It is very easy to get carried away with the excitement of a heated bidding session. Bid up to an odd number, £107 rather than £100, $207 rather than $200. Do not be afraid to shout this out if you are in with a chance as the bidding is closing. It may help you to pip a bid left by someone who was unable to attend. If you walk into an auction in progress and bid for an item which you have not carefully inspected, remember that it may not be as good as it appears from the back of the room.

If you sell items at auction agree on a realistic reserve. This is the lowest price for which you are prepared to sell the item. Take into account *all* the charges that will be subtracted from this. Strong interest from one buyer will only achieve your reserve. If several buyers are interested you may achieve an excellent price but this is by no means certain.

This writer has received hundreds of letters from owners of Lloyd Loom furniture with the perennial question 'How much is it worth?'. It is impossible to answer this question without detailed reference and a clear photograph. If you want to sell an item of special interest and you do not get the sort of response you want from an antique dealer, write to any of the specialists listed in the back of this book (page 160) for a valuation, that is, the price they would pay for the item. Always enclose a colour photograph and a stamped, addressed envelope for the reply. So much can be told from a photograph – colour, condition etc, all which effect its value – so it is essential to enclose one.

Right: A rare Lusty's model No. 32 armchair, 1927–41. One of Lusty's largest armchairs and used to furnish the observation lounge of the airship R100 (see book's endpapers). The model may have been commissioned especially for airship use. Light by comparison with most other types of furniture, the chair was given a generous width to allow passengers to sit comfortably whilst wearing their overcoats as airships were poorly heated. The model became popular with British RAF fighter pilots who, during the Battle of Britain, were kept waiting on alert for many hours wearing bulky flying garb. *Collection of the Anacara Company, Stamford CT, USA.*

INDEX

NOTE: Armchairs appear throughout the book to illustrate many aspects of Lloyd Loom furniture. They are therefore indexed by the aspect of design or the model they illustrate and only rare examples are listed under 'armchair'. Where illustrations appear on the same page as text reference they are not indexed separately.

A

advertising, *10–11*, 34, 36, 38, *40*, 136
armchairs *and see* chairs, models, suites, *6*, 34, *38–9, 66, 157*
art fibre, *7, 9*
assembly *and see* construction techniques, 54–9
Australian products, 23

B

baby carriages, *12, 13, 21, 26, 31–2*
Barbola, *36–7*, 62, 105, 115
Bauhaus, 81
bedside cabinets *and see* cupboards, 106–7
bentwood furniture, 45–6
binding, 139
blanket chests, 107
bookshelves, 101
braid, 9, 53, 139
  metal, 85
Breese, David and Kim, *58*

C

cabinets *and see* bedside cabinets, cupboards, 39
cake stands, *36–7, 58*, 111
chair makers, 54
chairs *and see* armchairs, models, suites, 68–9, *74–5*, 90, 138–9, *150–51*,
  cantilever, 80, 81, *82*, 141
  for children, 118–21
  dining, 98–9, *100*, 113
  easy, 70, 73
  invalid, 92, *93*
  legs, *22, 48*
  metal framed, *80*, 81–5, *137*
  nursing, 79, *106*
  rocking, *17, 25*, 70–71, *76, 77*, 81, *121*
chaise longue *and see* day beds, settees, 91–2

children's furniture, *28–9*, 62, 118–21
cleaning, 147–8
colours, 38, 61, 64, 148, *149*
construction techniques *and see* assembly, 9, 18–19, 48–9, 138–9
contract furniture, 36–7, 69–70, 74–5
cupboards *and see* bedside cabinets, cabinets, 28–9, 106–7
cushions *and see* upholstery, 46, 55, 56, 70

D

Dalrymple, Claude, 27
damage, 143–7
date stamps *and see* labels, 123–4
  Lusty's, 127–37
dating, 128, 138–41
day beds *and see* settees, 82–3, 90–93
decoration *and see* Barbola, braid, fitch work, Jacquard, stencil patterns, 38, *61*, 115, 121
  and dating, 139–41
  framework, 54
design *and see* models, 68, 70
desks, 100–101
Duval, René, 23

E

English products see Lusty, W. & Sons

F

feet-caps, 57, 139
ferneries *and see* plant stands, 68–9, 116–17, 120, *121*
ferrules, 57
fibre construction, *8*, 9, 18–21, 50–51
finishing, 60–64
fire screens, 115
fitch work, 38, 86, 87–9, *121*, 141

Flanders, Don, 41
frameworks, 45–9, 81, 141
French products, 23
fruit baskets, 111
Fulda factory, 24
Fussner, George, 24

G

German products, 24
Grand Rapids Fibre Co., 9

H

hampers, 102–4
hat stands, 112
Heywood-Wakefield Company, 21, 23, 41, *77*
  and labelling, 124–5

I

identification of Lloyd Loom furniture *and see* dating, 9

J

Jacquard, 51, *52*, 53, 73, *90–91*, 121, *135, 140*, 141

K

Klar, Elof, 24
Knutson, Clarence, *76–7*

L

labels *and see* date stamps, 123–4
  Lloyd's, *122*, 123–5
  Lusty's, 123, 127–37
lamps, *33, 39, 83, 106, 108*, 109–11, 120, *121*
Larsen, Lewis, 26, 68, 81
leg rests *and see* stools, 92
legs,
  cabriole, 79, *110*, 141
  chair, *22, 48*
  table, 85, 94, 139
  steel tubular, 46, 48

linen baskets, *28–9, 83, 102*, 103–4, *106–7, 136*
Lloyd, Marshall Burns, 9, 13–18, 21, 53, *85*
Lloyd Loom Furniture Ltd, 58
Lloyd Manufacturing Company, 13, 16, 18, 26–27
    factory, *18–19*, 27, 31, 41, *50, 54*
    labels, 123–5
    newspaper, 21, 24, 27
Lloyd Scale Company, 16
Lloyd-Sello Fibre Company, 24
Lloyd/Flanders, 41–2, *43*, 64–5
London and North Eastern Railway (L.N.E.R.), 36, *37*
looms, 50–51
Lusty, Frank, *30, 82*
Lusty, W. & Sons, 23, 24, 30–31, 34, 41, *64*
    factory, 31, 41
    labels and date stamps, 123, 127–37
Lusty, William K., *30*, 68

M
magazine racks, 112
marketing, 31–2
Mathisen, Kristian, 27
Menominee, *16*, 21
    factory, *18–19*, 27, 31, 41, *50, 54*
metal frames, *65, 80, 81–5, 137*, 141
models,
    All Square, 78
    Classics, 42, *43*, 64–5
    Country Club, *80, 81*
    Delux, *22*, 35–37, *40*, 46–7, *54, 70, 73, 74, 79, 92–3, 95, 96, 98–9, 113, 117*, 118–19, *120, 126, 129, 155*
    Heirloom, 42
    Jacobean, 77, *78, 96*
    Maid Saver, 39
    Pattern Weave, *52*

Popular, *52, 54, 55, 56, 61, 63, 70, 73, 75, 85*, 92, 118, *120, 135*, 141
    Reflections, 42
    Seaside, 81
    Traditions, 42
Mouronval, Pierre, 23
music boxes, 118–19

N
needlework boxes *and see* sewing baskets, *114*, 115

O
ottomans, 107
oxy-acetylene method, 16

P
painting, 60–61, 64, 148
paper, in manufacturing, 7, 19
patents, 7, 16, 19, 87, 131
Peterson, Hilda, 26–7
plant stands and planters *and see* ferneries, *28–9, 33, 70–71*, 116–17
prams *and see* baby carriages, *31–2*
product range *and see* models, 60–61, 67–70

R
R stamps, 128
rejects, 128
renovations, 144–8
    and date stamps, 127–8
repairs, 144–8
Royds, George, 34, 36, 38

S
settees *and see* day beds, *33*, 36–7, *64–5*, 68–71, *90–93, 118*
sewing baskets *and see* needlework boxes, *36–7*
Sheraton Toe, 78
show-wood frames, 61, *76, 77*, 78–9, 141

signatures, 124
skirts, *6, 22, 35, 54, 56, 63, 73, 155*
slipper box, 115
stamps *and see* date stamps, labels, 123–4
stencil patterns, *55, 62, 63, 83, 120*
stick fibre *see* fitch work
stools, *91*, 92, *106*, 113, *136*
suites *and see* chairs, settees, 72–3, 77–8

T
tables 28–9, 33–4, 37–9, 44, 64–5, *68–71, 83, 85*, 94–7, *106, 108, 110*
    children's, 119–20
    coffee, *40*, 96, *110*
    legs, *85*, 94, *139*
    Library, 100
tea trays, 111
tea waggons/trolleys, 111
Thonet, Michael, 45
trade marks, 32, *122*, 123–5
Tucker, H.C., 23

U
umbrella stands, 112
upholstery *and see* cushions, 57, 121
utility stamp, 134

V
value, 152–6
vases, *111*

W
Washburn and Heywood Chair Company, 21
wastepaper baskets, 36–7, 105
weave widths, 51
White, C.O., Company, 16
wicker working, 13–14, 18, *20*, 21
woodworm, 143
World's Fair, Chicago 1933, 39

USEFUL CONTACTS

The following lists some contacts that the reader may find useful but is by no means a complete guide to the companies or individuals who have an interest in this subject.

Manufacturers

Lloyd/Flanders
3010 Tenth Street
PO Box 550
Menominee, MI 49858
USA

Lloyd Loom of Spalding
Wardentree Lane
Pinchbeck
Spalding
Lincs PE11 3SY
England

W Lusty & Sons Ltd
Hoo Lane
Chipping Campden
Glos GL55 6AU
England

Vincent Sheppard NV
Industriepark Ijzeren Bareel 5
B-8587 Spiere
Belgium

Accente
Einrichtungsgesellschaft mbH
Viktoriastrasse 12-14
D-41747 Viersen
Germany

General Information
Collecting (buying or selling)

Paul Smith
21 Aldwick Gardens
Bognor-Regis
West Sussex PO21 3QT
England

Gail and Larry Melgary
Colonial Corner Antiques
1728 7th Street
Menominee, MI 49858
USA

Steve Fulford
Weathervane Antiques
1059 Marinette Avenue
Marinette, WI 54143
USA

Wilh Winkelman (BV)
de Winckelaer
Chr Huygensstrasse 3
3291 CR Stryen
Holland

Novantino AG
Drubergstrasse 16
8703 Erlenbach
Switzerland

Lee J Curtis
Wiener Platz 8
81667 Munich
Germany

Specialist Restoration

Paul Boulton
Burwash Post Office
East Sussex TN19 7EP
England
(Repairs, respraying – using Lusty's original colours)

Lloyd Loom of Spalding
Wardentree Lane
Pinchbeck
Spalding
Lincs PE11 3SY
England
(Supplies Lloyd Loom repair kits)